ALEXANDER-GRACE EDUCATION

CONTENTS

ALEXANDER-GRACE EDUCATION

Understanding the MAP Tests

The NWEA MAP (Measures of Academic Progress) test is an adaptive assessment that is designed to measure student growth and progress in a variety of subject areas. The test is taken by millions of students across the United States and is widely used by educators to help inform instruction and measure student outcomes. The NWEA MAP test is administered online and provides immediate feedback on student performance, allowing teachers to adjust their teaching strategies and provide targeted support to individual students.

The NWEA MAP test is unique in that it is adaptive, which means that the difficulty of the questions adjusts based on the student's responses. This allows the test to be more personalized to each student's abilities and provides a more accurate measure of their knowledge and skills. The test covers a range of subject areas, including mathematics, reading, language usage, and science, and is administered multiple times throughout the school year. This allows teachers to track student progress and growth over time and make data-driven decisions to improve student outcomes.

ALEXANDER-GRACE EDUCATION

Purpose and Benefits of MAP Testing

The primary purpose of the MAP Test is to provide valuable insights into a student's learning and academic progress. By offering a detailed analysis of a student's performance in reading, language usage, mathematics, and science, the test helps teachers tailor their instruction to meet individual needs. The MAP Test also serves as a benchmarking tool, allowing schools and districts to compare their students' performance with national norms and other local institutions.

This data-driven approach enables educators to make informed decisions about curriculum, instructional methods, and resource allocation, ultimately leading to improved student outcomes. Additionally, the MAP Test can help identify gifted students who may benefit from advanced or accelerated programs, as well as students who may require additional support or interventions.

Test Format and Content

The MAP Test is divided into four primary content areas: reading, language usage, mathematics, and science. Each section consists of multiple-choice questions that cover various topics and skills within the respective subject. The test is untimed, allowing students to work at their own pace and ensuring a lower level of test anxiety. The computer-adaptive nature of the MAP Test ensures that the difficulty of questions adjusts based on a student's performance, making it suitable for students of all ability levels. As a result, the MAP Test not only evaluates a student's mastery of grade-level content but also assesses their readiness for more advanced material.

Adaptive Testing and Scoring System

One of the unique aspects of the MAP Test is its adaptive testing system. As students answer questions, the test adjusts the difficulty of subsequent questions based on their performance. This adaptive nature allows the test to home in on a student's true ability level, providing more accurate and meaningful results. The MAP Test uses a RIT (Rasch Unit) scale to measure student achievement, which is an equal-interval scale that allows for easy comparison of scores across grade levels and subjects. This scoring system allows educators and parents to track a student's growth over time, making it an invaluable tool for understanding academic progress and setting individualized learning goals.

Preparing for Success on the MAP Test

Effective preparation for the MAP Test involves a combination of understanding the test format, mastering content knowledge, and developing test-taking strategies. This test prep book is designed to provide students with comprehensive guidance on each content area, offering targeted instruction and practice questions to build confidence and ensure success. Additionally, the book includes test-taking tips and strategies to help students approach the test with a calm and focused mindset. By working through this book and dedicating time to consistent practice, students will be well-equipped to excel on the MAP Test and achieve their academic goals.

Note that, since there is no cap to the level that a student can work to in preparation for this test, there is no 'completion' of content, as students can simply do questions from grades above in preparation. It should be noted that students are not expected to work far above grade level to succeed in this test, as consistent correct answers are more relevant.

ALEXANDER-GRACE EDUCATION

What Is Contained Within this Book?

Within this book you will find 320 questions based off content which would be found within the MAP test your student will take. The content found in this book will be the equivalent of grade 7 level. Note that since this test is adaptive, some students may benefit by looking at several grade levels of content, not just their own.

At the end of the book will contain answers alongside explanations. It is recommended to look and check your answers thoroughly in regular intervals to make sure you improve as similar questions come up.

ALEXANDER-GRACE EDUCATION

Topic 1 – Analyzing Allegories and Symbolism

In the quaint village of Willow Creek, the townspeople were preparing for the annual Harvest Festival. Among them was young Emily, who found a mysterious old book in her grandmother's attic. The book was filled with stories, each weaving intricate tales of heroes and mythical creatures. As she delved deeper, she realized that these were not just tales, but allegories reflecting the history and values of her village. Intrigued, Emily decided to explore these allegories, uncovering the hidden symbolism behind each story.

1.1) What does the mysterious old book in Emily's grandmother's attic symbolize?

☐ A guide to the Harvest Festival

☐ A map of Willow Creek

☐ The wisdom of past generations

☐ An ordinary storybook

1.2) How does the story of Willow Creek use allegory?

☐ By using heroes to represent village values

☐ By outlining the rules of the Harvest Festival

☐ By telling straightforward historical events

☐ By describing Emily's daily routine

1.3) What might the mythical creatures in the book represent?

☐ Real animals in the village

☐ Neighbors in Willow Creek

☐ Challenges or fears of the villagers

☐ Characters in a video game

ALEXANDER-GRACE EDUCATION

1.4) Why is Emily interested in the allegories in the book?

☐ To find a recipe for the festival

☐ To uncover hidden meanings about her village

☐ Just for entertainment

☐ To prepare for a school test

1.5) What can readers learn from analyzing allegories and symbolism in stories?

☐ Details of festival preparations

☐ Deeper meanings and moral lessons

☐ How to read faster

☐ Geographical knowledge of villages

In a distant land, a young boy named Leo discovered an ancient, talking tree in the forest. The tree, named Sage, shared stories from centuries ago, each a metaphor for the balance of nature and human life. Leo, fascinated, realized that these stories were more than just tales; they were symbolic lessons about the interconnectedness of all living things. Eager to learn more, Leo visited Sage every day, unraveling the profound wisdom hidden within these timeless allegories.

1.6) What does the talking tree, Sage, represent in the story?

☐ The wisdom of nature

☐ A character in a fairy tale

☐ A typical tree in the forest

☐ A guardian of the forest

1.7) How do Sage's stories serve as metaphors?

☐ Illustrating the balance between nature and humans

☐ Describing different types of trees

☐ Teaching about forest animals

☐ Telling the history of the forest

1.8) What lesson is Leo learning from the allegories told by Sage?

☐ How to identify different trees

☐ The history of his family

☐ Ways to navigate the forest

☐ The interconnectedness of all living things

1.9) What is the primary theme of the allegorical stories shared by Sage?

☐ The importance of tree conservation

☐ The relationship between nature and humanity

☐ Forest survival skills

☐ The adventure of exploring forests

1.10) Why are allegorical stories like Sage's important for students like Leo to learn?

☐ They are part of the school curriculum

☐ They provide entertainment

☐ They teach deeper moral and philosophical lessons

☐ They help in learning tree names

Sophie, a curious girl from a coastal town, stumbled upon a hidden cave while exploring the beach. Inside, she found murals depicting the sea and its creatures, each mural telling a story of harmony and conflict. These murals weren't just art; they were symbolic narratives about the relationship between the sea and human life. Sophie, intrigued by these visual allegories, began to interpret the deeper meanings, learning about the respect and care needed for the ocean and its inhabitants.

1.11) What do the murals in the cave symbolize?

☐ A history of the town

☐ The relationship between the sea and humans

☐ Just decorative art

☐ A map of the coastal area

1.12) How do the stories told by the murals serve as allegories?

☐ By illustrating a treasure hunt

☐ By telling about the town's founders

☐ By depicting a fictional underwater world

☐ By showing harmony and conflict between nature and humans

1.13) What lesson is Sophie learning from the murals?

☐ The importance of respecting the ocean

☐ Art techniques for mural painting

☐ Sea creature identification

☐ The history of her town

1.14) What is the primary theme of the murals?

☐ The science of marine biology

☐ Care and respect for the ocean and its creatures

☐ The fun of beach activities

☐ The adventure of sea exploration

1.15) Why are symbolic narratives like the cave murals important for students like Sophie?

☐ They are interesting stories

☐ They are part of the school curriculum

☐ They teach about environmental stewardship

☐ They help in geography classes

In a small mountain town, Alex discovered an old mural depicting a great eagle soaring above the landscape. This mural, a well-known town legend, was believed to represent freedom and the spirit of adventure. Each element in the mural, from the mountains to the eagle, symbolized aspects of the townsfolk's dreams and aspirations. Alex, intrigued by this legend, began to explore the symbolic meanings behind the mural, learning about the town's heritage and the importance of pursuing one's dreams.

1.16) What does the great eagle in the mural symbolize?

☐ A symbol of the town's sports team

☐ A character in a local story

☐ Freedom and adventure

☐ A common bird in the town

ALEXANDER-GRACE EDUCATION

1.17) How does the mural serve as a symbolic narrative?

☐ By showing the geography of the mountain

☐ By illustrating a typical day in the town

☐ By depicting historical events

☐ By representing the dreams and aspirations of the townsfolk

1.18) What lesson is Alex learning from the mural?

☐ The importance of pursuing dreams

☐ The history of the town

☐ Art techniques for mural creation

☐ Bird species identification

1.19) What is the primary theme of the town's mural?

☐ The spirit of adventure and chasing dreams

☐ The history of the town's founding

☐ The beauty of mountain landscapes

☐ The art of mural painting

1.20) Why are symbolic narratives like the town's mural important for students like Alex?

☐ They help in geography classes

☐ They are part of art class

☐ They provide entertainment

☐ They inspire understanding of cultural heritage and personal aspirations

In a bustling city, Eva, a young artist, found inspiration in the diverse cultures around her. She began creating a series of paintings, each illustrating different cultural tales and myths. These paintings were not just colorful depictions; they were rich in symbolism, reflecting the beliefs, traditions, and shared experiences of the various communities. Eva's art became a bridge, connecting people through the universal language of allegory and symbolism.

1.21) What do Eva's paintings symbolize in her city?

☐ Famous landmarks in the city

☐ The diversity of cultures and beliefs

☐ Just colorful cityscapes

☐ Eva's personal diary

1.22) How do Eva's paintings use allegory?

☐ By showing daily life in the city

☐ By illustrating modern city living

☐ By portraying historical figures

☐ By depicting cultural tales and myths

1.23) What lesson can be learned from Eva's approach to art?

☐ Basic painting techniques

☐ Famous artistic styles

☐ The power of art in bridging cultural gaps

☐ The history of the city

1.24) What is the primary theme of Eva's series of paintings?

☐ The beauty of urban life

☐ The history of art in the city

☐ The unity and diversity of cultural experiences

☐ The process of artistic creation

1.25) Why is it important for students to understand symbolic art like Eva's?

☐ It helps in appreciating cultural diversity and expression

☐ It is useful for geography lessons

☐ It makes it easier to understand city life

☐ It is essential for art class

In a small desert town, young Kai discovered an ancient scroll depicting a legendary phoenix. The scroll described the phoenix's cycle of rebirth, symbolizing renewal and transformation. Intrigued, Kai began to see this legend as a metaphor for his town's resilience in the harsh desert. He shared the story with his friends, sparking discussions about the importance of hope and perseverance.

1.26) What does the phoenix in the ancient scroll symbolize?

☐ A symbol of the town's history

☐ A common desert bird

☐ A fictional character

☐ Renewal and transformation

ALEXANDER-GRACE EDUCATION

1.27) How does the legend of the phoenix serve as a metaphor?

☐ For the geography of the desert

☐ For the town's resilience and hope

☐ For the life cycle of birds

☐ For the history of ancient civilizations

1.28) What lesson is Kai learning from the phoenix's story?

☐ Bird species identification

☐ Desert survival skills

☐ Ancient writing techniques

☐ The importance of hope and perseverance

1.29) What is the primary theme of the phoenix legend?

☐ Overcoming challenges and rebirth

☐ The beauty of the desert

☐ The art of scroll making

☐ Ancient mythological creatures

1.30) Why are allegorical stories like the phoenix important for students like Kai?

☐ They are part of history class

☐ They help in science studies

☐ They teach life lessons about resilience and hope

☐ They provide entertainment

In a futuristic city, Lara, a young inventor, created a robot named Orion. Orion was no ordinary robot; it was designed to interpret human emotions through art. Through Orion's paintings, Lara discovered unique perspectives on human feelings, each artwork acting as a window into the soul. These artworks were allegorical, symbolizing complex emotions in a way words never could. Lara's invention became a tool for understanding and empathy, bridging the gap between humans and machines.

1.31) What do Orion's paintings symbolize in the story?

☐ Human emotions and perspectives

☐ Just colorful abstract art

☐ The technology in the city

☐ Lara's personal diary

1.32) How does Orion use allegory in its paintings?

☐ By depicting landscapes

☐ By interpreting human emotions

☐ By showcasing technological advancements

☐ By portraying famous historical events

1.33) What lesson can be learned from Orion's artwork?

☐ Modern painting techniques

☐ Understanding and empathy through art

☐ The history of the futuristic city

☐ Robotics and artificial intelligence

1.34) What is the primary theme of Orion's series of paintings?

☐ The process of artistic creation

☐ The advancement of robotics

☐ The intersection of technology and human emotion

☐ The evolution of futuristic cities

1.35) Why is understanding allegorical art like Orion's important?

☐ It provides entertainment

☐ It fosters empathy and deeper emotional insight

☐ It is essential for studying robotics

☐ It helps in learning about future technologies

In a magical forest, a young explorer named Mia found a hidden garden with plants that whispered secrets. Each plant represented a different aspect of nature and life, sharing tales of growth, survival, and harmony. Mia realized these whispers were not just random; they were allegories, teaching her about the delicate balance of ecosystems and the interdependence of all living things. Her discovery became a journey of understanding the wisdom embedded in nature.

1.36) What do the whispering plants in the garden symbolize?

☐ Different aspects of nature and life

☐ Ordinary sounds of the forest

☐ Secrets of the magical forest

☐ Mia's imagination

1.37) How do the plants' tales serve as allegories?

☐ By teaching about ecosystems and interdependence

☐ By telling fictional stories about forest creatures

☐ By describing the process of photosynthesis

☐ By narrating the history of the forest

1.38) What lesson is Mia learning from the whispering plants?

☐ How to navigate a magical forest

☐ Gardening skills

☐ The scientific names of plants

☐ The wisdom of nature and the balance of ecosystems

1.39) What is the primary theme of the plants' whispers in the story?

☐ The adventure of exploring magical places

☐ Interdependence and balance in nature

☐ The folklore of the forest

☐ The art of gardening

1.40) Why are allegorical stories like the plants' whispers important?

☐ They help in learning about magical creatures

☐ They are part of botany studies

☐ They provide entertainment

☐ They teach about ecological balance and respect for nature

Topic 1 – Answers

Question Number	Answer	Explanation
1.1	The wisdom of past generations	The book symbolizes the wisdom of past generations as it contains stories that reflect the history and values of the village.
1.2	By using heroes to represent village values	The allegory is used to reflect village values through stories of heroes and mythical creatures.
1.3	Challenges or fears of the villagers	The mythical creatures likely represent the challenges or fears faced by the villagers.
1.4	To uncover hidden meanings about her village	Emily is interested in the allegories to uncover hidden symbolism about her village's history and values.
1.5	Deeper meanings and moral lessons	Readers can learn deeper meanings and moral lessons through the analysis of allegories and symbolism.
1.6	The wisdom of nature	Sage, the talking tree, represents the wisdom of nature through its stories.
1.7	Illustrating the balance between nature and humans	Sage's stories serve as metaphors for the balance of nature and human life.
1.8	The interconnectedness of all living things	Leo learns about the interconnectedness of all living things from Sage's allegories.
1.9	The relationship between nature and humanity	The primary theme of Sage's stories is the relationship between nature and humanity.
1.10	They teach deeper moral and philosophical lessons	Allegorical stories teach deeper moral and philosophical lessons about life and nature.
1.11	The relationship between the sea and humans	The murals symbolize the relationship between the sea and human life through their allegorical narratives.
1.12	By showing harmony and conflict between nature and humans	The murals use allegory to depict harmony and conflict between nature and humans.
1.13	The importance of respecting the ocean	Sophie learns the importance of respecting the ocean and its creatures from the murals.
1.14	Care and respect for the ocean and its creatures	The primary theme of the murals is the care and respect for the ocean and its inhabitants.
1.15	They teach about environmental stewardship	Symbolic narratives teach the importance of environmental stewardship and respect for nature.
1.16	Freedom and adventure	The great eagle symbolizes freedom and the spirit of adventure, representing the townsfolk's dreams and aspirations.
1.17	By representing the dreams and aspirations of the townsfolk	The mural serves as a symbolic narrative of the townsfolk's dreams and aspirations through its elements.
1.18	The importance of pursuing dreams	Alex learns about the importance of pursuing one's dreams from the mural's symbolism.

1.19	The spirit of adventure and chasing dreams	The primary theme of the mural is the spirit of adventure and the pursuit of dreams.
1.20	They inspire understanding of cultural heritage and personal aspirations	Symbolic narratives inspire an understanding of cultural heritage and personal aspirations.
1.21	The diversity of cultures and beliefs	Eva's paintings symbolize the diversity of cultures and beliefs in the city through allegorical tales and myths.
1.22	By depicting cultural tales and myths	Eva's paintings use allegory by illustrating cultural tales and myths to reflect community beliefs and experiences.
1.23	The power of art in bridging cultural gaps	Eva's approach teaches the power of art to bridge cultural gaps and connect diverse communities.
1.24	The unity and diversity of cultural experiences	The primary theme of Eva's paintings is the unity and diversity of cultural experiences.
1.25	It helps in appreciating cultural diversity and expression	Understanding symbolic art is important for appreciating cultural diversity and expression.
1.26	Renewal and transformation	The phoenix symbolizes renewal and transformation, reflecting the town's resilience in the desert.
1.27	For the town's resilience and hope	The legend serves as a metaphor for the town's resilience and hope through the phoenix's cycle of rebirth.
1.28	The importance of hope and perseverance	Kai learns the importance of hope and perseverance from the phoenix's story of rebirth.
1.29	Overcoming challenges and rebirth	The primary theme of the phoenix legend is overcoming challenges and experiencing rebirth.
1.30	They teach life lessons about resilience and hope	Allegorical stories teach important life lessons about resilience and hope in the face of adversity.
1.31	Human emotions and perspectives	Orion's paintings symbolize human emotions and perspectives, offering insight into the soul through art.
1.32	By interpreting human emotions	Orion uses allegory in its paintings by interpreting and representing human emotions artistically.
1.33	Understanding and empathy through art	Orion's artwork teaches the lesson of understanding and empathy through the allegorical representation of emotions.
1.34	The intersection of technology and human emotion	The primary theme of Orion's paintings is the intersection of technology and human emotion, exploring their relationship.
1.35	It fosters empathy and deeper emotional insight	Understanding allegorical art fosters empathy and deeper emotional insight, bridging human and technological understanding.
1.36	Different aspects of nature and life	The whispering plants symbolize different aspects of nature and life, sharing wisdom through their tales.
1.37	By teaching about ecosystems and interdependence	The plants' tales serve as allegories by teaching about ecosystems and the interdependence of living things.
1.38	The wisdom of nature and the balance of ecosystems	Mia learns about the wisdom of nature and the balance of ecosystems from the whispering plants.
1.39	Interdependence and balance in nature	The primary theme of the plants' whispers is the interdependence and balance within nature.
1.40	They teach about ecological balance and respect for nature	Allegorical stories like the plants' whispers teach the importance of ecological balance and respect for nature.

Topic 2 - Understanding Irony and Satire

In the small town of Winkleville, the mayor decided to host a "Serious Day" where everyone had to be solemn and serious for 24 hours. The local comedian, Mr. Chuckles, thought this was the perfect opportunity to spread joy. He walked around town, wearing a suit of armor made of spoons, claiming he was defending the town from the "dragon of gloominess." Surprisingly, his antics made even the stern Mayor laugh, turning "Serious Day" into an unexpected celebration of happiness and laughter. This turn of events left the townsfolk wondering if the mayor's original plan was a clever joke all along.

2.1) What is ironic about Mr. Chuckles' actions on Serious Day?

☐ He ended up making the day more joyful, contrary to the mayor's decree.

☐ He decided to leave town instead of participating.

☐ He was the only one who remained serious throughout the day.

☐ He actually found a real dragon in the town.

2.2) What could be considered satirical about the mayor's plan for a 'Serious Day'?

☐ Everyone in town was already very serious before the day.

☐ It suggests that the town has no real problems.

☐ It implies that joyfulness is not welcome in Winkleville.

☐ It mocks the idea that seriousness can be enforced to create order.

2.3) How did the townsfolk react to the unexpected turn of Serious Day?

☐ They demanded Mr. Chuckles to be punished for breaking the rules.

☐ They continued to be serious despite Mr. Chuckles' efforts.

☐ They left town to avoid participating.

☐ They enjoyed the day more than they anticipated.

2.4) What does Mr. Chuckles' suit of armor represent in the story?

☐ Serious preparation for an actual battle.

☐ A misunderstanding of the mayor's announcement.

☐ A humorous opposition to the gloominess enforced by the mayor.

☐ A traditional costume for celebrations in Winkleville.

2.5) What underlying message might the author be conveying through the story?

☐ The effectiveness of rules in maintaining order in society.

☐ The need for a real defense against external threats.

☐ The dangers of taking oneself too seriously.

☐ The importance of joy and laughter in bringing people together.

At Greenleaf School, the principal announced a new rule: homework must be done in complete silence to encourage concentration. The next day, a group of students, led by Jamie, decided to protest the rule in a unique way. They showed up to school dressed as mimes, complete with painted faces and striped shirts, and "silently" did their homework in the cafeteria. Their silent protest not only caught the attention of teachers and students alike but also sparked a school-wide debate about the best ways to study. By the end of the week, the principal decided to relax the rule, admitting that sometimes silence isn't golden after all.

2.6) What is ironic about the students' protest against the silence rule?

☐ They made a lot of noise to show that silence is necessary.

☐ They decided to do their homework at home instead of school.

☐ They used silence to protest a rule about being silent.

☐ They asked the principal to join their protest.

2.7) How does the students' mime protest serve as satire?

☐ It shows that the students prefer not to do homework at all.

☐ It implies that all school rules are unnecessary.

☐ It suggests that the school is always too loud.

☐ It criticizes the rule by exaggerating the concept of silence.

2.8) What was the outcome of the students' silent protest?

☐ The students were punished for not following the rule.

☐ The principal relaxed the homework silence rule.

☐ Homework was banned at Greenleaf School.

☐ The school day was made longer to ensure quiet study time.

2.9) What message might the author be trying to convey with the story of the mime protest?

☐ Open communication and creativity can lead to positive changes.

☐ Silence is always the best policy for effective learning.

☐ Rules are made to be broken by students.

☐ Studying in complete silence is the most effective method.

2.10) Why did the protest spark a school-wide debate?

☐ It challenged the effectiveness of studying in complete silence.

☐ It led to a discussion about banning all school rules.

☐ It proposed a new uniform for the school.

☐ It suggested that all homework should be done in mime outfits.

When the local library announced it was banning all comic books to promote "serious reading," a group of students led by Alex decided to take action. They started a "serious reading" club that exclusively read and discussed the most extravagant and fantastical comic books they could find. Their club quickly became the most popular after-school activity, drawing attention from students of all ages who found joy and excitement in the vivid stories and artwork of the comics. The librarian, seeing the enthusiasm and engagement the club inspired, eventually lifted the ban, recognizing the value of all forms of reading in sparking creativity and learning.

2.11) What is ironic about the 'serious reading' club's choice of literature?

☐ They chose the most serious books available to show their support for the ban.

☐ They avoided reading altogether, focusing on discussions instead.

☐ They read comic books to protest a ban on them, despite the club's name.

☐ They read only non-fiction books to comply with the ban.

2.12) How does the formation of the club serve as a satirical response to the library's ban?

☐ It indicates that students were not reading before the club was formed.

☐ It implies that all bans in libraries are effective.

☐ It suggests that the library was previously lacking in engaging activities.

☐ It mocks the ban by showing that comic books can also be serious literature.

2.13) What was the librarian's reaction to the club's popularity?

☐ The ban on comic books was lifted, acknowledging their educational value.

☐ No changes were made; the ban remained in place.

☐ The librarian decided to ban all books to ensure fairness.

☐ The librarian joined the club as its most active member.

2.14) What message might the author be trying to convey with the story?

☐ Libraries should not offer activities that are too fun.

☐ Serious reading clubs are necessary for proper education.

☐ All forms of reading, including comic books, can be valuable and educational.

☐ Bans on certain types of books are always beneficial.

2.15) Why did the 'serious reading' club become so popular?

☐ It offered a creative and enjoyable way to challenge the ban.

☐ It was the only after-school activity available.

☐ It was supported by famous authors.

☐ It provided free comic books to all members.

The town of Whispering Pines decided to save water by banning the use of garden hoses, prompting residents to find alternative ways to water their gardens. In response, Mr. Green, an avid gardener, set up an elaborate system of rain barrels and small, hand-held watering cans to keep his garden thriving. His garden became so lush and vibrant that it won the town's "Best Garden" award. The irony was not lost on the town officials, who had initially feared that gardens would suffer under the new rule. Instead, Mr. Green's success inspired the whole town to adopt more sustainable gardening practices.

2.16) What is ironic about Mr. Green's response to the garden hose ban?

☐ He managed to create the best garden in town despite the restriction.

☐ He used even more water with his new system than before.

☐ He decided to remove his garden altogether.

☐ He protested the ban by not watering his garden at all.

ALEXANDER-GRACE EDUCATION

2.17) How does Mr. Green's garden success serve as a satire on the hose ban?

☐ It highlights the effectiveness of alternative, sustainable gardening methods.

☐ It indicates that the ban was unnecessary from the start.

☐ It shows that bans can sometimes lead to better outcomes.

☐ It suggests that the town's officials were not knowledgeable about gardening.

2.18) What was the town's reaction to Mr. Green's award-winning garden?

☐ They were inspired to adopt more sustainable gardening practices.

☐ They implemented stricter water usage rules.

☐ They awarded Mr. Green with a lifetime supply of water.

☐ They decided to lift the ban on garden hoses immediately.

2.19) What message might the author be trying to convey with this story?

☐ Innovation and adaptation can lead to unexpected positive outcomes.

☐ Strict rules always result in public dissatisfaction.

☐ Awards are the most important aspect of gardening.

☐ Gardening without hoses is the only sustainable method.

2.20) Why did the town officials initially fear the garden hose ban?

☐ They feared an increase in water use from other sources.

☐ They worried about the impact on the town's water bill.

☐ They thought gardens would suffer and lose their beauty.

☐ They were concerned about a backlash from the community.

In a twist of fate, the town of Giggleswick, known for its quiet and reserved community, decided to host an "Opposite Day." On this day, everyone was encouraged to act contrary to their usual behavior. Mrs. Featherstone, the town's most notorious quiet librarian, surprised everyone by leading a loud and lively parade through the town center, complete with a marching band and cheerleaders. Her transformation from a reserved librarian to the life of the party became the highlight of the day, sparking conversations about the joy of stepping out of one's comfort zone. The event was such a success that it became an annual tradition, making "Opposite Day" the most anticipated day of the year in Giggleswick.

2.21) What is ironic about Mrs. Featherstone's actions on Opposite Day?

☐ She decided to leave town for the day to avoid participating.

☐ She protested Opposite Day by being even quieter than usual.

☐ The quiet librarian became the most lively person in town.

☐ She organized a silent reading session instead of a parade.

2.22) How does Opposite Day in Giggleswick serve as satire?

☐ It implies that such events are a waste of time and resources.

☐ It suggests that the town is always too loud and needs to be quieter.

☐ It mocks the town's usually reserved nature by celebrating its opposite.

☐ It shows that traditions cannot be changed.

2.23) What was the outcome of Mrs. Featherstone leading the parade?

☐ The town decided to cancel all future Opposite Days.

☐ She moved away from Giggleswick due to embarrassment.

☐ She was asked to resign from her job as a librarian.

☐ Opposite Day became an annual tradition in Giggleswick.

2.24) What message might the author be trying to convey with the story?

☐ Librarians should not participate in public events.

☐ Embracing change and trying new things can lead to positive community traditions.

☐ Quiet people should always strive to be the center of attention.

☐ Loud celebrations are the only way to unite a community.

2.25) Why did Opposite Day become so popular in Giggleswick?

☐ It allowed residents to explore different aspects of their personalities.

☐ The town was usually boring, with no other events happening.

☐ It was the only day of the year when noise was allowed in the town.

☐ Everyone enjoyed seeing Mrs. Featherstone out of her usual role.

In an effort to promote health and fitness, the city of Breezydale announced a "Car-Free Day," where residents were encouraged to use alternative forms of transportation. Mr. Treadwell, known for his love of vintage cars, took the announcement as a challenge and arrived downtown on a horse, claiming it was his "new environmentally friendly vehicle." His humorous approach not only garnered smiles but also sparked a discussion on the importance of sustainable transportation options. By the end of the day, the streets of Breezydale were filled with bicycles, skateboards, and even a few more horses, turning "Car-Free Day" into a celebration of community and creativity.

2.26) What is ironic about Mr. Treadwell's choice of transportation on Car-Free Day?

☐ He used his car, ignoring the city's announcement.

☐ He chose a horse, highlighting the contrast between old and new forms of transport.

☐ He invented a new form of environmentally friendly vehicle.

☐ He walked to downtown instead of using any transportation.

2.27) How does Car-Free Day in Breezydale serve as satire?

☐ It suggests that cars are the only viable form of transportation.

☐ It implies that the city usually does not care about the environment.

☐ It uses humor to promote a serious message about sustainable transportation.

☐ It shows that such initiatives are not taken seriously by the residents.

2.28) What was the community's reaction to Car-Free Day?

☐ The day was ultimately deemed a failure due to low participation.

☐ It led to a wide variety of creative transportation choices being used.

☐ The city decided to make every day car-free moving forward.

☐ Residents protested against the inconvenience caused.

2.29) What message might the author be trying to convey with this story?

☐ People are resistant to change, especially when it involves transportation.

☐ Community initiatives can be successful when approached with creativity and humor.

☐ Older forms of transportation are always superior to modern ones.

☐ Environmental initiatives are often viewed as humorous or not serious.

2.30) Why did 'Car-Free Day' become a celebration of community and creativity?

☐ People enjoyed the novelty of seeing horses on city streets.

☐ The event was accompanied by a large festival.

☐ Residents embraced the challenge and explored diverse transportation methods.

☐ It was the first time the city had tried to reduce car usage.

In the village of Littlebrook, a new law was passed requiring all pets to be kept on leashes at all times, even cats. Mrs. Whiskers, the village cat lady, found this rule absurd for her ten free-spirited felines. Instead of leashes, she crafted tiny, decorative hats for each cat, arguing they were "leash alternatives." Surprisingly, the village council was amused and intrigued by her creativity, leading to a revision of the law to allow for "creative alternatives to leashes." Littlebrook soon became famous for its uniquely adorned pets, attracting tourists from far and wide to see the spectacle.

2.31) What is ironic about Mrs. Whiskers' solution to the leash law?

- ☐ She moved out of Littlebrook to avoid following the law.

- ☐ She trained her cats to walk on leashes like dogs.

- ☐ She complied with the law in an unexpected way by using hats instead of leashes.

- ☐ She started a petition to completely abolish the law.

2.32) How does the village council's reaction to the hats serve as satire?

- ☐ It mocks the rigidity of laws by accepting an unconventional compliance method.

- ☐ It suggests that the law was never meant to be taken seriously.

- ☐ It shows that the council members are easily swayed by public opinion.

- ☐ It implies that all village laws are decided based on amusement value.

2.33) What was the outcome of the 'creative alternatives to leashes' law?

- ☐ The villagers protested against the absurdity of the new law.

- ☐ Littlebrook became known for its uniquely adorned pets, drawing in tourists.

- ☐ Other villages started to enforce stricter leash laws in response.

- ☐ Mrs. Whiskers was elected as the new head of the village council.

2.34) What message might the author be trying to convey with the story?

☐ Tourism is the most important aspect of a village's economy.

☐ Creativity and flexibility can lead to positive and unexpected outcomes.

☐ Laws should be strictly followed without room for interpretation.

☐ Cats should not be kept as pets in villages.

2.35) Why did Littlebrook's new law attract tourists?

☐ The village offered tours to show off the leashed pets.

☐ The spectacle of pets with creative adornments was unique and entertaining.

☐ Tourists were interested in the village's strict pet laws.

☐ Mrs. Whiskers became a celebrity, drawing people to visit.

After years of peaceful coexistence, the town of Merryfield was surprised to wake up to a decree from Mayor Goodwin stating that all houses must be painted green to "blend in with nature." The Peterson family, known for their bright pink house, decided to comply in their own way. They added green stripes to their pink house, creating a watermelon pattern. The quirky design became an instant hit, leading to a wave of creative house painting across Merryfield. Mayor Goodwin, initially baffled, eventually embraced the diversity, declaring Merryfield the "most colorful town in the state."

2.36) What is ironic about the Peterson family's response to the mayor's decree?

☐ They refused to paint their house at all, defying the mayor's orders.

☐ They moved out of Merryfield to avoid compliance.

☐ They painted their house entirely green, exactly as the decree specified.

☐ They turned the decree into an opportunity for creativity, contrary to its intent.

2.37) How does the town's reaction to the Petersons' house serve as satire?

☐ It highlights the absurdity of enforcing uniformity through a decree.

☐ It implies that all houses in Merryfield were previously green.

☐ It shows that the mayor's decrees are usually ignored by the townspeople.

☐ It suggests that Merryfield residents always wanted more colorful houses.

2.38) What was Mayor Goodwin's reaction to the wave of creative house painting?

☐ He resigned as mayor, overwhelmed by the townspeople's creativity.

☐ He issued another decree to reverse the painting trend.

☐ He embraced the diversity, celebrating Merryfield's newfound colorfulness.

☐ He fined the Peterson family for starting the trend.

2.39) What message might the author be trying to convey with this story?

☐ Townspeople should seek approval before expressing creativity.

☐ Uniformity can stifle creativity, and diversity should be celebrated.

☐ Painting houses in bright colors can lead to legal troubles.

☐ Decrees from authority should always be followed without question.

2.40) Why did Merryfield become known as the 'most colorful town in the state'?

☐ The Petersons' creative compliance inspired a town-wide trend of colorful houses.

☐ The town hosted a painting competition that attracted artists nationwide.

☐ A mistake at the paint factory resulted in a surplus of colorful paint.

☐ The mayor's decree was misunderstood, leading to varied interpretations.

Topic 2 - Answers

Question Number	Answer	Explanation
.1	He ended up making the day more joyful, contrary to the mayor's decree.	Mr. Chuckles used humor on a day meant for seriousness, ironically making it joyful.
.2	It mocks the idea that seriousness can be enforced to create order.	The mayor's plan is satirical as it suggests enforcing seriousness could improve order, mocking over-regulation.
.3	They enjoyed the day more than they anticipated.	The townsfolk's positive reaction to the humor on Serious Day was unexpected and joyful.
.4	A humorous opposition to the gloominess enforced by the mayor.	The suit of armor made of spoons represents a playful and humorous defiance against the enforced solemnity.
.5	The importance of joy and laughter in bringing people together.	The story conveys that laughter and joy are essential for unity and happiness, despite attempts to suppress them.
.6	They used silence to protest a rule about being silent.	The irony lies in the students using silence, the very thing the rule enforced, as a form of protest.
.7	It criticizes the rule by exaggerating the concept of silence.	The mime protest serves as satire by exaggerating silence to critique the effectiveness and reasonableness of the homework rule.
.8	The principal relaxed the homework silence rule.	The outcome of the protest was a change in policy, showing the effectiveness of the students' silent demonstration.
.9	Open communication and creativity can lead to positive changes.	The mime protest story suggests that creative expression and dialogue can influence policy and foster a more inclusive environment.
.10	It challenged the effectiveness of studying in complete silence.	The protest sparked debate by questioning whether silence truly aids concentration, leading to a reconsideration of the rule.
.11	They read comic books to protest a ban on them, despite the club's name.	The irony is in the club's focus on comic books, which were banned, under the guise of 'serious reading.'
.12	It mocks the ban by showing that comic books can also be serious literature.	The club satirically responds to the ban by demonstrating that comic books have educational value, challenging the ban's premise.
.13	The ban on comic books was lifted, acknowledging their educational value.	The librarian's positive response to the club's popularity and the educational engagement it spurred led to the lifting of the ban.
.14	All forms of reading, including comic books, can be valuable and educational.	The story conveys the message that diverse forms of literature, like comic books, can contribute to learning and creativity.
.15	It offered a creative and enjoyable way to challenge the ban.	The club's popularity stemmed from its enjoyable and innovative approach to protesting the comic book ban.
.16	He managed to create the best garden in town despite the restriction.	The irony is in Mr. Green's success in creating a lush garden without a hose, contrary to the town officials' fears.
.17	It highlights the effectiveness of alternative, sustainable gardening methods.	Mr. Green's success serves as a satirical commentary on the hose ban by proving alternative methods can be superior.
.18	They were inspired to adopt more sustainable gardening practices.	The town's positive reaction to Mr. Green's garden inspired a community-wide shift towards sustainable gardening.
.19	Innovation and adaptation can lead to unexpected positive outcomes.	This story illustrates how creativity and adaptability in response to restrictions can result in beneficial and innovative solutions.

2.20	They thought gardens would suffer and lose their beauty.	The town officials' initial fear was that the ban on hoses would negatively impact the aesthetic and health of gardens.
2.21	The quiet librarian became the most lively person in town.	The irony lies in Mrs. Featherstone's transformation from a quiet librarian to leading a lively parade on Opposite Day.
2.22	It mocks the town's usually reserved nature by celebrating its opposite.	Opposite Day serves as satire by encouraging behaviors contrary to Giggleswick's norm, highlighting the joy in diversity of actions.
2.23	Opposite Day became an annual tradition in Giggleswick.	Mrs. Featherstone's unexpected participation led to the establishment of Opposite Day as a cherished local tradition.
2.24	Embracing change and trying new things can lead to positive community traditions.	The story suggests that stepping out of one's comfort zone, as Mrs. Featherstone did, can foster community spirit and new traditions.
2.25	It allowed residents to explore different aspects of their personalities.	Opposite Day's popularity stemmed from giving residents a sanctioned opportunity to behave in uncharacteristically vibrant ways.
2.26	He chose a horse, highlighting the contrast between old and new forms of transport.	Mr. Treadwell's ironic choice of a horse as a "new environmentally friendly vehicle" playfully emphasizes sustainable transport.
2.27	It uses humor to promote a serious message about sustainable transportation.	Car-Free Day serves as satire by using Mr. Treadwell's humorous approach to underscore the importance of exploring sustainable transit options.
2.28	It led to a wide variety of creative transportation choices being used.	The community's enthusiastic and imaginative response to Car-Free Day showcased the potential for diverse and sustainable transport.
2.29	Community initiatives can be successful when approached with creativity and humor.	The story conveys that engaging the community with humor and creativity can effectively promote important environmental goals.
2.30	Residents embraced the challenge and explored diverse transportation methods.	Car-Free Day became a celebration due to the community's creative embrace of alternative transportation, fostering unity and innovation.
2.31	She complied with the law in an unexpected way by using hats instead of leashes.	Mrs. Whiskers' creative compliance with the leash law using hats instead highlights the irony in her literal yet innovative approach.
2.32	It mocks the rigidity of laws by accepting an unconventional compliance method.	The council's amused acceptance of "leash alternatives" satirizes the initial law's rigidity by endorsing creativity over strict adherence.
2.33	Littlebrook became known for its uniquely adorned pets, drawing in tourists.	The outcome of adopting "creative alternatives to leashes" transformed Littlebrook into a tourist attraction for its adorned pets.
2.34	Creativity and flexibility can lead to positive and unexpected outcomes.	This story illustrates that flexible thinking and creative problem-solving can transform challenges into opportunities for innovation.
2.35	The spectacle of pets with creative adornments was unique and entertaining.	Littlebrook's law attracted tourists due to the unique and visually appealing spectacle of creatively adorned pets.
2.36	They turned the decree into an opportunity for creativity, contrary to its intent.	The Peterson family's creative response to the green house decree ironically fostered a wave of creativity, subverting its original intent.
2.37	It highlights the absurdity of enforcing uniformity through a decree.	The reaction to the Petersons' house serves as satire by showing how attempts at uniformity can instead spark creativity and diversity.
2.38	He embraced the diversity, celebrating Merryfield's newfound colorfulness.	Mayor Goodwin's positive response to the creative house painting trend reflects an acceptance of diversity and creativity.
2.39	Uniformity can stifle creativity, and diversity should be celebrated.	The story conveys that attempts at enforcing uniformity can unintentionally inspire creativity, highlighting the value of diversity.
2.40	The Petersons' creative compliance inspired a town-wide trend of colorful houses.	Merryfield's recognition as the "most colorful town" stemmed from the community embracing and expanding upon the Petersons' creative idea.

Topic 3 - Exploring Literary Elements

In the mystical land of Azuria, a young dragon named Ember discovered a hidden talent for painting. Ember's paintings were not just beautiful; they had the magical ability to make anyone who looked at them feel peaceful and happy. However, the dragon elders did not believe in art; they thought dragons should focus on flying and fire-breathing. Determined to share her gift, Ember organized an exhibition in the village square. To everyone's surprise, the paintings brought joy not only to the dragons but also to the creatures of Azuria, bridging the gap between them.

3.1) What is the main theme of the story?

☐ The importance of pursuing one's passion despite opposition.

☐ The necessity of fire-breathing for dragons.

☐ How to organize an art exhibition.

☐ The dangers of ignoring traditional dragon activities.

3.2) What tone does the story primarily convey?

☐ Inspirational, highlighting Ember's journey to acceptance.

☐ Angry, emphasizing the conflict between Ember and the elders.

☐ Sad, focusing on the elders' disapproval of Ember's art.

☐ Fearful, detailing the dangers of Azuria's mystical land.

3.3) How does Ember's voice contribute to the story's meaning?

☐ It argues against the value of art in society.

☐ It shows the power of determination and the impact of sharing one's talents.

☐ It demonstrates the elders' wisdom in discouraging artistic pursuits.

☐ It narrates the history of Azuria without focusing on personal experiences.

3.4) How does the story's setting enhance its theme?

☐ It shows that art is not valued in dragon society.

☐ It indicates that dragons are naturally talented painters.

☐ The setting is irrelevant to the story's theme.

☐ The mystical land of Azuria adds a magical quality to Ember's artistic talents.

3.5) What literary element is used to show Ember's impact on Azuria?

☐ Metaphor, comparing Ember to a famous artist.

☐ Imagery, through the description of Ember's paintings and their effects.

☐ Simile, by saying Ember's art is like a bright light in Azuria.

☐ Personification, giving human characteristics to Ember's paintings.

Luna, a young witch in training, was tasked with brewing a potion to cure laughter. The more she tried, the funnier her failures became, causing even more laughter among her friends. In an unexpected twist, Luna discovered that laughter was the true cure to sadness in her village. Her potion experiments turned into comedy shows, where villagers gathered not for a cure, but for the joy and laughter Luna's efforts brought them. Eventually, Luna became known as the greatest healer, not with potions, but with her infectious laughter.

3.6) What is the main theme of Luna's story?

☐ Finding joy in unexpected places and the healing power of laughter.

☐ The importance of serious study over having fun.

☐ How to become a successful comedian.

☐ The challenges of witchcraft and potion brewing.

3.7) How does the tone of Luna's story contribute to its message?

☐ Angry, depicting the villagers' initial dissatisfaction with Luna.

☐ Frustrated, focusing on Luna's inability to brew the potion.

☐ Light-hearted and amusing, it underscores the unexpected joys of life.

☐ Sombre and serious, highlighting the difficulties Luna faces.

3.8) Which literary element is most evident in Luna's potion experiments?

☐ Foreshadowing, hinting at Luna's future as a comedian.

☐ Alliteration, to make the descriptions more engaging.

☐ Irony, as her failure to create a serious potion leads to joy.

☐ Hyperbole, exaggerating the effects of the failed potions.

3.9) How does the setting affect the story?

☐ It emphasizes the traditional nature of the village.

☐ It is irrelevant; the story could happen anywhere.

☐ It makes the story less believable and difficult to follow.

☐ It creates a magical backdrop that makes Luna's discoveries more impactful.

3.10) What does Luna's transition from witch to comedian illustrate?

☐ The decline in traditional magical practices.

☐ The villagers' lack of appreciation for potion brewing.

☐ The failure of witchcraft to address real problems.

☐ Adaptability and finding one's true calling in unexpected places.

The town of Windmore was famous for its annual kite festival, where everyone competed to see whose kite could fly the highest. This year, a young inventor named Theo decided to enter with a kite he designed to change colors with the altitude. As Theo's kite ascended, it shifted through a rainbow of colors, dazzling the onlookers and judges alike. The spectacle brought the community together, reminding everyone that the festival was not just about competition but also about innovation, beauty, and shared enjoyment. Theo's kite didn't just win the contest; it won the hearts of Windmore.

3.11) What is the central theme of Theo's kite story?

☐ Inventing new things is a waste of time.

☐ Kites should only be flown for fun, not in contests.

☐ Innovation and creativity can transform traditional events into new experiences.

☐ Competitions are only about winning.

ALEXANDER-GRACE EDUCATION

3.12) How does the story's setting contribute to its theme?

☐ The setting is insignificant; the story could happen anywhere.

☐ Windmore's kite festival provides the perfect backdrop for showcasing innovation.

☐ The town of Windmore is against new ideas.

☐ The story emphasizes the harsh weather conditions in Windmore.

3.13) Which literary element is most prominent in describing Theo's kite?

☐ Symbolism, representing Theo's growth as an inventor.

☐ Metaphor, comparing the kite to a bird.

☐ Alliteration, to enhance the description of the kite.

☐ Imagery, vividly painting the kite's color-changing journey through the sky.

3.14) What tone does the story of Theo's kite primarily convey?

☐ Boredom, highlighting the monotony of annual festivals.

☐ Anger, due to the competitive nature of the festival.

☐ Disappointment, focusing on the challenges Theo faces.

☐ Wonder and excitement, as the kite's performance captivates the town.

3.15) How does Theo's invention impact the community of Windmore?

☐ It leads to jealousy and competition among other participants.

☐ It inspires a sense of unity and appreciation for creativity among the townsfolk.

☐ It causes the festival to be canceled due to safety concerns.

☐ It has no significant impact; life in Windmore remains the same.

In the bustling city of Technoville, a group of students embarked on a project to build a robot that could paint. Named Artie, the robot quickly became a local sensation for its unique art style, which combined elements of abstract and realism. Artie's creations were not only visually stunning but also sparked discussions about the nature of creativity and whether a machine could possess a true artistic spirit. The students' project challenged the community's perceptions of art and technology, leading to a broader conversation about the future of creativity.

3.16) What is the central theme of the story about Artie the robot?

☐ The intersection of technology and creativity challenges traditional views on art.

☐ Robots will eventually replace human artists.

☐ Technology is incapable of understanding abstract concepts.

☐ Artistic talent is innate and cannot be replicated by machines.

3.17) How does the setting of Technoville enhance the story?

☐ It distracts from the story's focus on creativity.

☐ It suggests that the residents are skeptical of new technologies.

☐ It underscores the theme of innovation in a community known for embracing technology.

☐ It implies that such a project could not succeed in a less advanced city.

3.18) Which literary element is used to describe Artie's art style?

☐ Metaphor, likening Artie's creations to a new art movement.

☐ Imagery, providing vivid descriptions of Artie's blend of abstract and realism.

☐ Personification, attributing human qualities to the robot and its art.

☐ Simile, comparing Artie's art to famous human artists.

3.19) What tone does the story convey about the future of creativity?

☐ Indifferent, suggesting that technology has little impact on art.

☐ Pessimistic, fearing that machines will overshadow human creativity.

☐ Confused, reflecting uncertainty about the role of technology in art.

☐ Optimistic and curious, exploring the potential of new forms of artistic expression.

3.20) How does Artie's story impact the community's view on art?

☐ It leads to a rejection of traditional art forms.

☐ It causes a divide between supporters of traditional art and advocates for technological innovation.

☐ It broadens their perspective, encouraging openness to innovation in artistic expression.

☐ It has no effect; the community remains indifferent to Artie's art.

In the forest of Whispering Willows, a curious fox named Felix stumbled upon an ancient spellbook hidden beneath a pile of autumn leaves. Felix, who had always dreamed of performing magic, began to study the spellbook with great enthusiasm. To his amazement, he discovered he could speak to the trees, which shared secrets of the forest's past and tales of forgotten magic. Felix's new abilities allowed him to become a guardian of the forest, protecting it from those who sought to harm it. His bond with the forest and its inhabitants grew stronger, turning Felix into a legend among the woodland creatures.

3.21) What is the main theme of Felix's adventure?

☐ How to become a magician.

☐ The superiority of foxes over other forest animals.

☐ The power of curiosity and the importance of protecting nature.

☐ The dangers of meddling with ancient magic.

3.22) How does the ability to speak to trees change Felix?

☐ It has no significant impact; Felix remains the same.

☐ It makes him arrogant, believing he is the most powerful creature in the forest.

☐ It isolates him from other animals who cannot understand the trees.

☐ It transforms him into a guardian of the forest, highlighting his growth and responsibility.

3.23) Which literary element is most evident in the description of the forest's past?

☐ Symbolism, with the forest representing the mystery of nature.

☐ Imagery, as the tales from the trees paint vivid pictures of the forest's history.

☐ Allusion, referencing well-known myths and legends.

☐ Onomatopoeia, using sounds to bring the forest's past to life.

3.24) What tone is primarily conveyed through Felix's interactions with the forest?

☐ Wonder and awe, as Felix discovers the magic and history of the forest.

☐ Fear and suspense, as Felix uncovers the dangers lurking in the forest.

☐ Irritation, as Felix struggles with his new responsibilities.

☐ Boredom, suggesting that Felix finds the forest's secrets mundane.

3.25) How does the story illustrate the concept of unity with nature?

☐ By showing the conflict between Felix and the forest.

☐ Through Felix's role as a guardian, demonstrating a harmonious relationship between a creature and its environment.

☐ By suggesting that magic is the only way to truly understand nature.

☐ By depicting the forest as a dangerous place that must be conquered.

In the small seaside town of Coral Cove, a mysterious lighthouse began to glow every night, casting magical colors across the sky. The townspeople were puzzled, as the lighthouse had been abandoned for years. A young girl named Clara, driven by curiosity, decided to investigate. Inside, she discovered a hidden library filled with books on ancient maritime legends and spells. With the help of these books, Clara learned that the lighthouse was a beacon for lost sea creatures, guiding them to safety. She took it upon herself to maintain the lighthouse, becoming a guardian of both the sea and its mythical inhabitants.

3.26) What is the primary theme of the story set in Coral Cove?

- ☐ The importance of curiosity and the role of guardianship in protecting the natural and mythical world.
- ☐ The fear of the unknown and the dangers of exploring abandoned places.
- ☐ The process of maintaining a lighthouse.
- ☐ The loneliness of living in a small seaside town.

3.27) How does Clara's discovery in the lighthouse affect the plot?

- ☐ It leads to the closure of the lighthouse due to safety concerns.
- ☐ It has no significant impact on the story.
- ☐ It causes Clara to become isolated from the townspeople.
- ☐ It reveals the magical purpose of the lighthouse, shifting the story towards her role as its guardian.

3.28) Which literary element is used to describe the lighthouse's effect on the sky?

- ☐ Hyperbole, exaggerating the brightness and reach of the lighthouse's light.
- ☐ Metaphor, comparing the lighthouse's glow to a painter's brush.
- ☐ Personification, giving the lighthouse human-like qualities in its role.
- ☐ Imagery, vividly depicting the magical colors cast by the lighthouse across the sky.

3.29) What tone is established through the townspeople's reaction to the lighthouse?

- ☐ Mystery and wonder, as they are intrigued by the lighthouse's sudden activity.
- ☐ Panic, fearing the lighthouse's glow signifies danger.
- ☐ Indifference, showing little interest in the lighthouse's glow.
- ☐ Annoyance, upset by the disturbance caused by the light.

3.30) How does the story illustrate the connection between humans and the mythical?

☐ By revealing that the sea creatures were just a figment of Clara's imagination.

☐ Through Clara's role as the guardian, bridging the gap between the townspeople and the sea's mythical creatures.

☐ By suggesting that all myths are based on fear of the unknown.

☐ By showing that humans and mythical creatures cannot coexist peacefully.

Every winter, the village of Frostvale held a festival to celebrate the first snowfall, but one year, the snow did not come. The villagers, worried about the break in tradition, turned to Ava, a young weather mage in training. Ava, determined to save the festival, embarked on a quest to find the Snow Crystal, a mythical artifact said to control the weather. After a journey filled with challenges, Ava discovered the crystal in a hidden ice cave and used it to bring snow to Frostvale. The festival was a success, and Ava was hailed as a hero, her actions reminding everyone of the importance of resilience and hope.

3.31) What is the main theme of Ava's quest?

☐ The superiority of magic over nature.

☐ The importance of perseverance and hope in overcoming challenges.

☐ How to become a weather mage.

☐ The dangers of meddling with the weather.

3.32) How does the setting of Frostvale contribute to the story's mood?

☐ It detracts from the story's focus on Ava's quest.

☐ It suggests that the village is indifferent to the festival.

☐ It creates a sense of urgency and anticipation for the first snowfall, enhancing the story's mood of hope.

☐ It makes the story feel isolated and lonely.

3.33) Which literary element is most evident in Ava's discovery of the Snow Crystal?

☐ Irony, as the crystal was never needed to bring snow to Frostvale.

☐ Alliteration, to enhance the sound of the narrative.

☐ Symbolism, with the Snow Crystal representing hope and renewal.

☐ Imagery, describing the hidden ice cave and the crystal in vivid detail.

3.34) What tone does the story primarily convey?

☐ Indifferent, suggesting that the outcome of Ava's quest is unimportant.

☐ Comical, making light of the villagers' concern over the festival.

☐ Gloomy and despairing, focusing on the village's fear of a snowless winter.

☐ Adventurous and hopeful, highlighting Ava's determination to save the festival.

3.35) How does Ava's journey impact Frostvale?

☐ It has no lasting effect; the villagers quickly forget her contributions.

☐ It renews the villagers' spirit and faith in the power of community and magic.

☐ It leads to a ban on all future weather magic.

☐ It causes the villagers to become overly reliant on Ava for weather-related issues.

The town of Harmony was known for its silent nights, but this tranquility was shattered when a mysterious musician appeared, playing enchanting melodies that kept the townsfolk awake. Named Melody, she claimed her music could heal any sorrow. Despite initial resistance, the people of Harmony began to listen and found solace in her tunes. Melody's presence transformed the town, turning its silent nights into a symphony of comfort and hope. The once quiet town became a beacon for those seeking peace through music, and Melody was celebrated as Harmony's unsung hero.

3.36) What is the central theme of Melody's story in Harmony?

- ☐ The importance of maintaining silence.

- ☐ The disruption caused by new arrivals in a peaceful town.

- ☐ The process of becoming a professional musician.

- ☐ The transformative power of music and its ability to bring comfort and unity.

3.37) How does Melody's music change the town of Harmony?

- ☐ It leads to Harmony becoming deserted, as people seek quieter places.

- ☐ It causes conflict among the townsfolk, divided over the loss of silence.

- ☐ It brings the community together, offering solace and healing through her melodies.

- ☐ It has no effect; the townsfolk continue to value silence over music.

3.38) Which literary element is used to describe the effect of Melody's music?

- ☐ Imagery, creating vivid pictures of the town's transformation through sound.

- ☐ Metaphor, comparing Melody's music to a healing balm.

- ☐ Hyperbole, exaggerating the impact of the music on the town.

- ☐ Onomatopoeia, using sound words to mimic the music.

3.39) What tone does the story primarily convey?

- ☐ Uplifting and hopeful, emphasizing the positive change Melody brings to Harmony.

- ☐ Irritated, highlighting the townspeople's initial annoyance with Melody.

- ☐ Indifferent, suggesting that music is not a significant factor in the town's life.

- ☐ Melancholic, focusing on the town's struggle with the change.

3.40) How does the story illustrate the impact of art on society?

☐ By indicating that art is less important than traditional values like silence.

☐ By suggesting that art can be a source of division and unrest.

☐ By demonstrating that art's impact is limited to those who create it.

☐ By showing how Melody's music healed and united a community, highlighting art's role in social well-being.

Topic 3 - Answers

Question Number	Answer	Explanation
3.1	The importance of pursuing one's passion despite opposition.	Ember's journey emphasizes the value of following one's passion, even when faced with skepticism from traditional perspectives.
3.2	Inspirational, highlighting Ember's journey to acceptance.	The story is framed in an inspirational tone, showcasing Ember's determination to share her unique talent against the odds.
3.3	It shows the power of determination and the impact of sharing one's talents.	Ember's voice and actions demonstrate the significance of perseverance and sharing one's gifts for the greater good.
3.4	The mystical land of Azuria adds a magical quality to Ember's artistic talents.	The setting enhances the theme by adding a magical dimension to Ember's talent, showing that her art transcends ordinary abilities.
3.5	Imagery, through the description of Ember's paintings and their effects.	The use of vivid imagery to describe Ember's paintings illustrates the transformative impact of her art on the audience.
3.6	Finding joy in unexpected places and the healing power of laughter.	Luna's story centers on discovering happiness in unforeseen circumstances and the therapeutic effect of laughter.
3.7	Light-hearted and amusing, it underscores the unexpected joys of life.	The tone is amusing and light-hearted, reflecting the joy and laughter that Luna brings to her village despite initial failures.
3.8	Irony, as her failure to create a serious potion leads to joy.	The irony in Luna's failed potion experiments inadvertently becoming a source of happiness captures the essence of her story.
3.9	It creates a magical backdrop that makes Luna's discoveries more impactful.	The magical setting of the village enhances the whimsical and enchanting nature of Luna's journey and discoveries.
3.10	Adaptability and finding one's true calling in unexpected places.	Luna's transformation from a witch in training to a provider of joy through laughter illustrates adaptability and self-discovery.
3.11	Innovation and creativity can transform traditional events into new experiences.	Theo's story highlights how creativity and innovation can rejuvenate and add depth to traditional community events.
3.12	Windmore's kite festival provides the perfect backdrop for showcasing innovation.	The setting of the kite festival in Windmore is integral to the theme, emphasizing the community's embrace of Theo's creativity.
3.13	Imagery, vividly painting the kite's color-changing journey through the sky.	The use of detailed imagery to describe Theo's kite enhances the story's visual appeal and the wonder it inspires.
3.14	Wonder and excitement, as the kite's performance captivates the town.	The story conveys a tone of wonder and excitement, focusing on the community's admiration for Theo's innovative kite.
3.15	It inspires a sense of unity and appreciation for creativity among the townsfolk.	Theo's kite becomes a symbol of innovation, bringing the community together and fostering a collective appreciation for creativity.
3.16	The intersection of technology and creativity challenges traditional views on art.	The story explores how the blend of technology and creativity with Artie the robot opens new perspectives on artistic expression.
3.17	It underscores the theme of innovation in a community known for embracing technology.	Technoville's setting highlights its receptiveness to technological advances, enhancing the narrative of creativity and innovation.
3.18	Imagery, providing vivid descriptions of Artie's blend of abstract and realism.	The detailed imagery used to describe Artie's art style illustrates the unique fusion of techniques that spark community dialogue.

ALEXANDER-GRACE EDUCATION

3.19	Optimistic and curious, exploring the potential of new forms of artistic expression.	The story adopts an optimistic tone about the evolving relationship between art and technology, reflecting a forward-looking viewpoint.
3.20	It broadens their perspective, encouraging openness to innovation in artistic expression.	Artie's contributions lead to a wider acceptance and curiosity about the possibilities of integrating technology with art.
3.21	The power of curiosity and the importance of protecting nature.	Felix's story emphasizes the significance of curiosity in discovering one's abilities and the responsibility to protect nature.
3.22	It transforms him into a guardian of the forest, highlighting his growth and responsibility.	Felix's newfound communication with trees marks his evolution from a curious fox to a protector of the forest, showing personal growth.
3.23	Imagery, as the tales from the trees paint vivid pictures of the forest's history.	The use of detailed imagery to convey the stories of the forest's past enriches the narrative and Felix's connection to nature.
3.24	Wonder and awe, as Felix discovers the magic and history of the forest.	Felix's interactions with the forest are characterized by a sense of wonder, reflecting his awe at the magic and secrets he uncovers.
3.25	Through Felix's role as a guardian, demonstrating a harmonious relationship between a creature and its environment.	Felix's guardianship illustrates a deep bond with nature, showcasing a model of coexistence and mutual respect.
3.26	The importance of curiosity and the role of guardianship in protecting the natural and mythical world.	Clara's story underscores the value of curiosity in uncovering hidden truths and the significance of safeguarding both natural and mythical realms.
3.27	It reveals the magical purpose of the lighthouse, shifting the story towards her role as its guardian.	Clara's discovery inside the lighthouse changes the narrative direction, focusing on her new role as a protector of sea creatures.
3.28	Imagery, vividly depicting the magical colors cast by the lighthouse across the sky.	The use of vivid imagery to describe the lighthouse's effect enhances the magical and enchanting atmosphere of the story.
3.29	Mystery and wonder, as they are intrigued by the lighthouse's sudden activity.	The townspeople's reaction introduces a tone of mystery and fascination, drawing them into the unfolding magical phenomenon.
3.30	Through Clara's role as the guardian, bridging the gap between the townspeople and the sea's mythical creatures.	Clara's guardianship of the lighthouse symbolizes the connection between humans and mythical beings, fostering understanding and protection.
3.31	The importance of perseverance and hope in overcoming challenges.	Ava's quest for the Snow Crystal highlights the themes of determination and optimism in facing obstacles to achieve a communal goal.
3.32	It creates a sense of urgency and anticipation for the first snowfall, enhancing the story's mood of hope.	The setting of Frostvale, awaiting its first snowfall, amplifies the story's tension and the hopeful anticipation surrounding Ava's quest.
3.33	Symbolism, with the Snow Crystal representing hope and renewal.	The Snow Crystal symbolizes the essence of hope and the potential for new beginnings, central to the narrative's resolution.
3.34	Adventurous and hopeful, highlighting Ava's determination to save the festival.	The story conveys a tone of adventure, underscored by hope, as Ava embarks on her quest to ensure the festival's continuation.
3.35	It renews the villagers' spirit and faith in the power of community and magic.	Ava's successful quest revitalizes Frostvale's communal spirit, demonstrating the impact of individual courage on collective morale.
3.36	The transformative power of music and its ability to bring comfort and unity.	Melody's story in Harmony illustrates how music can heal, unite, and transform a community, transcending its previous silence.
3.37	It brings the community together, offering solace and healing through her melodies.	Melody's music alters the fabric of Harmony, transitioning it from a place of silence to one of communal healing and connection.
3.38	Imagery, creating vivid pictures of the town's transformation through sound.	The descriptive imagery used to depict Melody's music emphasizes the profound and healing impact it has on Harmony.
3.39	Uplifting and hopeful, emphasizing the positive change Melody brings to Harmony.	The story adopts an uplifting tone, celebrating the unifying and therapeutic effects of Melody's musical talents on the town.
3.40	By showing how Melody's music healed and united a community, highlighting art's role in social well-being.	Melody's influence on Harmony showcases the essential role of art in healing, unifying, and enhancing societal health and happiness.

Topic 4 - Characterization and Motivation

In the bustling city of Newburg, Sam, a young aspiring detective, was determined to solve the mystery of the missing golden statue from the city museum. Despite doubts from others due to his age, Sam's keen observation skills and determination led him to uncover clues overlooked by others. His investigation revealed a network of secrets entwined within the heart of Newburg. Along the way, Sam's courage inspired his skeptical peers, turning them into allies. In the end, Sam not only found the statue but also earned the respect of the community, proving that age is just a number when it comes to solving mysteries.

4.1) How does Sam's determination affect his character development?

- ☐ It causes him to give up on the investigation halfway through.
- ☐ It leads to reckless decisions that jeopardize the investigation.
- ☐ It drives him to overcome obstacles and skepticism, highlighting his growth into a respected detective.
- ☐ It isolates him from his peers, making him a loner.

4.2) What motivates Sam to solve the mystery of the missing statue?

- ☐ A desire to leave Newburg and start anew elsewhere.
- ☐ His aspiration to be a detective and to prove himself capable despite his youth.
- ☐ The promise of a financial reward.
- ☐ Peer pressure to fit in with his friends.

4.3) How do Sam's relationships change over the course of the story?

- ☐ His relationships deteriorate as he becomes more absorbed in the investigation.
- ☐ Initially met with skepticism, his peers come to support and respect him as he demonstrates his skills.
- ☐ He makes no new relationships, focusing solely on the mystery.
- ☐ He becomes estranged from his family who disapprove of his detective work.

4.4) What evidence from the text supports Sam's keen observation skills?

☐ He uncovers clues overlooked by others, leading to the discovery of the statue.

☐ He is described as having a photographic memory.

☐ He wins a detective trivia contest.

☐ He memorizes the entire city map in one night.

4.5) What does the resolution of the mystery reveal about Sam's character?

☐ It suggests that he is destined for a career outside of detective work.

☐ It indicates that he relies too heavily on others to solve problems.

☐ It shows that he was lucky rather than skilled.

☐ His success demonstrates his intelligence, courage, and the ability to inspire those around him.

Ellie, a shy student who loved writing, was challenged by her teacher to enter the school's annual poetry contest. Feeling out of her depth, Ellie doubted her abilities but found inspiration in the quiet moments of her day-to-day life. As she began to write, her confidence grew, and her poems reflected the beauty she saw in the world around her. Her final piece, a heartfelt ode to the simplicity of nature, won the contest. Through this experience, Ellie discovered her voice and learned that sharing her perspective could touch the hearts of others, encouraging her to keep writing.

4.6) What motivates Ellie to participate in the poetry contest?

☐ Her teacher's challenge and her own desire to find her voice through poetry.

☐ The promise of a cash prize for the winner.

☐ Peer pressure from her classmates.

☐ A requirement for passing her English class.

4.7) How does Ellie's character change throughout the story?

- ☐ Her character remains static; she does not change.

- ☐ She becomes disillusioned with writing and decides to pursue other interests.

- ☐ She becomes more introverted, preferring to write than interact with others.

- ☐ She transitions from being shy and doubtful to confident in her ability to express herself.

4.8) What evidence from the text supports Ellie's growth as a writer?

- ☐ Her increasing confidence is reflected in her poems, culminating in a contest-winning piece.

- ☐ She receives a letter of commendation from a famous poet.

- ☐ She starts a blog to share her poems with a wider audience.

- ☐ Her teacher praises her for her improvement in class discussions.

4.9) How do Ellie's poems impact her peers and teachers?

- ☐ They are moved by the beauty and sincerity of her perspective, showing the impact of sharing one's voice.

- ☐ Her work is criticized for not adhering to traditional poetic forms.

- ☐ They encourage her to focus on more practical subjects instead of poetry.

- ☐ Her peers and teachers do not understand her poems, feeling they are too complex.

4.10) What does Ellie's victory in the contest reveal about her character?

- ☐ It highlights her creativity, resilience, and the value of staying true to oneself.

- ☐ It reveals her competitive nature and desire to outdo her classmates.

- ☐ It suggests that success in contests is the only measure of a writer's worth.

- ☐ It indicates that she may have compromised her values to win.

ALEXANDER-GRACE EDUCATION

n the small village of Greenwood, Marco, a young baker, dreamed of creating a recipe that would bring the whole community together. Despite facing criticism for his unconventional ideas, Marco persevered. He experimented with flavors from around the world, blending them into traditional breads. His creation, a loaf infused with spices and herbs representing the diverse backgrounds of Greenwood's residents, was a hit at the village fair. Marco's bread not only won the baking contest but also sparked conversations among villagers, celebrating their differences and fostering a newfound sense of unity.

4.11) What drives Marco to create a new recipe?

☐ A desire to prove his critics wrong by winning a competition.

☐ His desire to unite the community and celebrate its diversity through his baking.

☐ The need to uphold his family's baking tradition.

☐ The potential fame and profit from winning the baking contest.

4.12) How does Marco's character develop in response to criticism?

☐ He becomes resentful towards the villagers for their lack of support.

☐ He starts to doubt his skills and the value of his creative ideas.

☐ He considers giving up baking entirely due to the negativity.

☐ He becomes more determined and innovative, using the criticism as motivation to improve.

4.13) What role does Marco's bread play in the story?

☐ It causes jealousy among other bakers in the village.

☐ It serves as a symbol of unity and diversity, bringing the villagers together.

☐ It is a minor detail that does not significantly impact the plot.

☐ It leads to a disaster at the village fair, ruining Marco's reputation.

4.14) How do the villagers' perceptions of Marco change by the end of the story?

☐ Their perceptions do not change; they continue to see him as an outsider.

☐ They remain skeptical of his unconventional baking methods.

☐ They become more critical of his work, preferring traditional recipes.

☐ They come to appreciate his creativity and the way he embraces the village's diversity.

4.15) What message does the story convey about innovation and tradition?

☐ It argues that tradition always outweighs innovation.

☐ It suggests that innovation can honor and enhance tradition, enriching community bonds.

☐ It warns against straying too far from traditional methods.

☐ It indicates that innovation is not welcomed in small communities.

Leo, known in his town for his incredible gardening skills, faced his biggest challenge yet: reviving the community garden, which had been neglected for years. His friends doubted the garden could ever bloom again, but Leo saw potential in the overgrown weeds and wilted flowers. With patience and care, he began to transform the space. Surprisingly, as the garden began to flourish, so did the community's spirit. Leo's dedication inspired his neighbors to join in, turning the garden into a vibrant oasis of colors and scents. The garden became a symbol of hope and renewal, reflecting Leo's belief that with love and effort, growth is always possible.

4.16) What motivates Leo to revive the community garden?

☐ The promise of a reward from the town council.

☐ A competition with a rival gardener.

☐ Peer pressure from his friends.

☐ His passion for gardening and his belief in the garden's potential to unite the community.

4.17) How does Leo's character influence the story's outcome?

☐ His initial enthusiasm fades, leaving the garden unfinished.

☐ His competitive nature alienates him from the community.

☐ His optimism and hard work lead to the transformation of the garden and the community's engagement.

☐ He relies on others to do the work, taking credit for their efforts.

4.18) What does the revival of the garden symbolize in the story?

☐ Hope and the positive impact of community collaboration and dedication.

☐ The community's dependency on a single individual for improvement.

☐ The temporary nature of beauty and success.

☐ Leo's desire for recognition and fame.

4.19) How do the community's views on the garden change?

☐ From skepticism to enthusiasm, as they witness the garden's transformation and Leo's dedication.

☐ Their initial support turns to disappointment when the garden does not meet their expectations.

☐ They become more critical of gardening as a worthwhile endeavor.

☐ They remain indifferent, despite the garden's revival.

4.20) What lesson does Leo's experience with the garden teach?

☐ That success in gardening is based on luck rather than skill.

☐ The power of perseverance and the value of nurturing growth, both in nature and within a community.

☐ The futility of trying to change something that has been neglected for too long.

☐ That community projects are not worth the effort.

In the town of Starlight, an annual talent show brought the community together, but no one ever expected the quiet librarian, Mrs. Jenkins, to sign up. Known for her reserved nature, Mrs. Jenkins surprised everyone by revealing her hidden talent: a beautiful singing voice. Her song, a melody about Starlight's history and the bonds within the community, moved the audience to tears. This performance changed the townspeople's perception of Mrs. Jenkins, showcasing the idea that everyone has hidden depths waiting to be discovered. Mrs. Jenkins became a local legend, reminding everyone that it's never too late to share your gifts with the world.

4.21) What is the main theme of Mrs. Jenkins' story?

- ☐ The discovery of hidden talents and the transformative power of sharing those talents with others.
- ☐ The reluctance of communities to accept change.
- ☐ The importance of talent shows in small communities.
- ☐ The fear of public speaking and performance.

4.22) How does Mrs. Jenkins' performance impact her relationship with the community?

- ☐ It causes jealousy among other talented townspeople.
- ☐ It leads to a newfound respect and admiration, as they see her in a new light.
- ☐ It has no impact; the townspeople continue to see her only as a librarian.
- ☐ It leads to increased expectations for her to perform regularly.

4.23) Which literary element is most evident in the description of Mrs. Jenkins' song?

- ☐ Alliteration, to enhance the lyrical quality of the song's description.
- ☐ Imagery, as the song vividly brings to life the history and unity of Starlight.
- ☐ Irony, because singing about the town's history contradicts her quiet personality.
- ☐ Metaphor, comparing Starlight's bonds to the melody of a song.

4.24) What does Mrs. Jenkins' decision to participate in the talent show reveal about her character?

☐ Uncertainty about her role within the community.

☐ A hidden desire for fame and recognition.

☐ Courage and a desire to connect with others on a deeper level, despite her usual reserve.

☐ A competitive nature, seeking to outdo others' talents.

4.25) How does the story challenge stereotypes about librarians?

☐ It implies that librarians' primary identity should be tied to their profession.

☐ By illustrating that librarians, like Mrs. Jenkins, can possess unexpected and remarkable talents beyond their professional roles.

☐ It reinforces the stereotype that librarians are always quiet and reserved.

☐ It suggests that all librarians have musical talents.

Tim, a young inventor in the town of Inventoria, was known for his wild and ambitious projects that never quite worked out. Despite his failures, Tim never lost his spirit or his passion for creating. His latest project was his most ambitious yet: a machine designed to clean the town's river, which had become polluted over the years. Many were skeptical, but Tim's dedication was unwavering. Against all odds, the machine worked perfectly, purifying the water and reviving the river's ecosystem. Tim's invention not only transformed the river but also changed how the townspeople viewed him and the potential of innovation to solve pressing environmental issues.

4.26) What drives Tim to continue inventing despite his past failures?

☐ Pressure from his family to succeed.

☐ His unwavering passion for innovation and his desire to make a positive impact on his community.

☐ The promise of fame and financial reward.

☐ Competition with another inventor in the town.

4.27) How does Tim's latest project affect his standing in the community?

☐ It leads to jealousy and rivalry among his peers.

☐ It has no impact; the townspeople remain indifferent to his achievements.

☐ It isolates him further due to the townspeople's skepticism.

☐ It earns him respect and admiration as his invention successfully addresses a significant environmental problem.

4.28) Which literary element is most prominent in the story's portrayal of Tim's invention?

☐ Hyperbole, exaggerating the effectiveness of the invention.

☐ Imagery, describing the transformation of the polluted river into a thriving ecosystem.

☐ Irony, highlighting the success of Tim's invention after a series of failures.

☐ Personification, giving the river human-like qualities of recovery and gratitude.

4.29) What theme is explored through Tim's journey and the river's revival?

☐ The inevitability of failure in the face of complex problems.

☐ The unimportance of community support in achieving one's goals.

☐ The superiority of natural methods over technological solutions.

☐ Perseverance and the impact of individual contributions towards solving environmental issues.

4.30) How does the story challenge the notion of failure?

☐ It portrays failure as something to be avoided at all costs.

☐ It indicates that success is only possible with external validation.

☐ It suggests that failure is an endpoint, not a step towards success.

☐ By showing that past failures can lead to significant achievements, emphasizing learning and growth.

In a small coastal town, Alex, a retired sailor, spent his days sharing tales of the sea with anyone who would listen. Though most people in town enjoyed his stories, some younger residents saw Alex as nothing more than an old man clinging to the past. Determined to change their minds, Alex decided to build a small boat to teach the youth about sailing, the sea, and the lessons it teaches about life. To everyone's surprise, these sailing lessons became the most anticipated activity of the summer. Through this experience, the younger generation gained a new respect for Alex and the wisdom he offered, bridging the gap between the old and the young.

4.31) What motivates Alex to share his tales and teach sailing?

☐ The need to prove his relevance to the town.

☐ The hope of returning to his life at sea.

☐ His desire to pass on his knowledge and to connect with the younger generation on a deeper level.

☐ The wish to start a business teaching sailing.

4.32) How does the community's perception of Alex change by the end of the story?

☐ There is no change; they continue to see him only as a retired sailor.

☐ From viewing him as an old man stuck in the past to recognizing him as a valuable source of wisdom and mentorship.

☐ Their initial admiration turns into annoyance with his constant storytelling.

☐ They become more dismissive of his stories and lessons.

4.33) Which literary element is most evident in Alex's building of the boat?

☐ Metaphor, comparing life lessons to navigating the sea.

☐ Foreshadowing, hinting at the success of his summer sailing lessons.

☐ Hyperbole, exaggerating the boat's impact on the town.

☐ Symbolism, with the boat representing Alex's journey to bridge generational divides.

4.34) What theme is explored through Alex's interaction with the youth?

☐ The superiority of older generations over the younger.

☐ The insignificance of past experiences in the modern world.

☐ The challenges of teaching traditional skills to disinterested youth.

☐ The value of intergenerational learning and the enduring relevance of life's experiences.

4.35) How does the story illustrate the impact of personal passions on a community?

☐ By showing how Alex's passion for the sea and sailing inspired and unified the community, particularly the youth.

☐ It suggests personal passions are often misunderstood and undervalued by others.

☐ It portrays personal hobbies as a distraction from more serious community issues.

☐ It indicates that individual interests have little effect on communal dynamics.

In the vibrant town of Melodiville, music was the soul of the community, but one genre was notably absent: jazz. Mia, a talented pianist with a deep love for jazz, noticed this gap. Despite jazz being unpopular in Melodiville, she was determined to introduce it to her town. Organizing a small jazz concert in the local park, Mia faced criticism and doubt. However, her performance mesmerized the audience, introducing them to the emotional depth and complexity of jazz. Mia's concert became a turning point for Melodiville, sparking a newfound appreciation for diverse musical genres and inspiring other musicians to explore and share their unique styles.

4.36) What motivates Mia to introduce jazz to Melodiville?

☐ The chance to win a prize in a music competition.

☐ The opportunity to become famous and recognized.

☐ A bet with a friend about changing the town's musical tastes.

☐ Her love for jazz and her desire to share its beauty with her community.

4.37) How does Mia's character influence the outcome of the story?

☐ Her competitive nature turns her peers against her.

☐ Her passion and perseverance lead to a successful concert that changes the town's musical landscape.

☐ Her fear of criticism nearly prevents the concert from happening.

☐ Her lack of preparation results in a poorly received performance.

4.38) Which literary element is most prominent in Mia's jazz concert?

☐ Alliteration, to enhance the musical quality of the narrative.

☐ Irony, as the town that lacked jazz becomes a hub for it.

☐ Metaphor, comparing jazz to a vibrant color palette.

☐ Imagery, describing the atmosphere of the park and the audience's reaction to the music.

4.39) What theme is explored through Mia's experience?

☐ The inevitable failure of introducing new ideas to traditional communities.

☐ The struggle of artists to gain recognition in their hometowns.

☐ The impact of sharing one's passion and the importance of cultural diversity in art.

☐ The conflict between different musical genres.

4.40) How does the story challenge the community's perception of music?

☐ By demonstrating that exposure to unfamiliar genres like jazz can enrich a community's cultural experience.

☐ It suggests the community was narrow-minded and resistant to change.

☐ It shows that only classical music is truly valued in Melodiville.

☐ It indicates that music is not a significant part of the town's identity.

Topic 4 - Answers

Question Number	Answer	Explanation
4.1	It drives him to overcome obstacles and skepticism, highlighting his growth into a respected detective.	Sam's determination showcases his character development from a doubted youth to a respected figure in solving the mystery.
4.2	His aspiration to be a detective and to prove himself capable despite his youth.	Sam is motivated by his dream of being a detective and proving that age does not limit one's capabilities in solving mysteries.
4.3	Initially met with skepticism, his peers come to support and respect him as he demonstrates his skills.	The change in Sam's relationships illustrates how his persistence and success in solving the mystery earn him respect and support.
4.4	He uncovers clues overlooked by others, leading to the discovery of the statue.	This evidence showcases Sam's keen observation skills, which are crucial to his success in solving the mystery.
4.5	His success demonstrates his intelligence, courage, and the ability to inspire those around him.	The resolution of the mystery highlights Sam's qualities, proving his worth and changing the community's perception of him.
4.6	Her teacher's challenge and her own desire to find her voice through poetry.	Ellie's motivation stems from the encouragement of her teacher and her personal journey to express herself through poetry.
4.7	She transitions from being shy and doubtful to confident in her ability to express herself.	Ellie's character development is marked by growing confidence and self-expression, culminating in her success in the poetry contest.
4.8	Her increasing confidence is reflected in her poems, culminating in a contest-winning piece.	Ellie's growth as a writer is evidenced by the evolution of her poetry, reflecting her personal journey and newfound confidence.
4.9	They are moved by the beauty and sincerity of her perspective, showing the impact of sharing one's voice.	Ellie's poems impact her audience by conveying her unique view of the world, demonstrating the power of authentic expression.
4.10	It highlights her creativity, resilience, and the value of staying true to oneself.	Ellie's victory reveals her inner strength, creativity, and the importance of genuine self-expression.
4.11	His desire to unite the community and celebrate its diversity through his baking.	Marco's drive to create a new recipe is inspired by his desire to reflect and celebrate the community's diverse culture.
4.12	He becomes more determined and innovative, using the criticism as motivation to improve.	Marco's response to criticism shows his resilience and creativity, leading to the success of his multicultural bread.

4.13	It serves as a symbol of unity and diversity, bringing the villagers together.	Marco's bread symbolizes the blending of diverse cultures and fosters a sense of community unity.
4.14	They come to appreciate his creativity and the way he embraces the village's diversity.	By the story's end, the villagers recognize Marco's contribution to celebrating their diversity through his innovative baking.
4.15	It suggests that innovation can honor and enhance tradition, enriching community bonds.	The story conveys that new ideas, like Marco's recipe, can strengthen and add depth to traditional community values.
4.16	His passion for gardening and his belief in the garden's potential to unite the community.	Leo's motivation is rooted in his love for gardening and his vision of the community garden as a unifying force.
4.17	His optimism and hard work lead to the transformation of the garden and the community's engagement.	Leo's character and efforts are pivotal in revitalizing the garden, which in turn inspires community participation and renewal.
4.18	Hope and the positive impact of community collaboration and dedication.	The garden's revival symbolizes hope and illustrates how collective effort and dedication can lead to positive change.
4.19	From skepticism to enthusiasm, as they witness the garden's transformation and Leo's dedication.	The community's perception shifts positively as they see the tangible results of Leo's dedication to the garden project.
4.20	The power of perseverance and the value of nurturing growth, both in nature and within a community.	Leo's experience teaches the importance of dedication and the transformative potential of care and effort in communal projects.
4.21	The discovery of hidden talents and the transformative power of sharing those talents with others.	Mrs. Jenkins' story explores the theme of uncovering and sharing one's hidden talents, leading to personal and communal transformation.
4.22	It leads to a newfound respect and admiration, as they see her in a new light.	Mrs. Jenkins' unexpected talent changes the community's perception, highlighting the depth and potential within everyone.
4.23	Imagery, as the song vividly brings to life the history and unity of Starlight.	The use of imagery in describing Mrs. Jenkins' song emphasizes the emotional and unifying power of her music
4.24	Courage and a desire to connect with others on a deeper level, despite her usual reserve.	Mrs. Jenkins' decision to perform reflects her inner strength and her wish to forge deeper connections with her community.
4.25	By illustrating that librarians, like Mrs. Jenkins, can possess unexpected and remarkable talents beyond their professional roles.	The story challenges stereotypes by showing that individuals often have multifaceted talents and interests beyond their job titles.
4.26	His unwavering passion for innovation and his desire to make a positive impact on his community.	Tim's continued efforts in invention, despite past failures, are driven by his love for creating and improving his community's environment.
4.27	It earns him respect and admiration as his invention successfully addresses a significant environmental problem.	Tim's successful project alters his community's perception, recognizing him as a valuable innovator and problem-solver.

4.28	Imagery, describing the transformation of the polluted river into a thriving ecosystem.	The detailed imagery used to depict the effect of Tim's invention on the river highlights the story's focus on environmental rejuvenation.
4.29	Perseverance and the impact of individual contributions towards solving environmental issues.	Tim's story emphasizes the theme of determination and the significant role individuals can play in addressing and solving environmental challenges.
4.30	By showing that past failures can lead to significant achievements, emphasizing learning and growth.	The narrative illustrates how previous setbacks are part of a learning process that can eventually lead to success and innovation.
4.31	His desire to pass on his knowledge and to connect with the younger generation on a deeper level.	Alex's motivation lies in his wish to share his experiences and wisdom, fostering a deeper understanding and connection with the youth.
4.32	From viewing him as an old man stuck in the past to recognizing him as a valuable source of wisdom and mentorship.	Alex's initiative to teach sailing transforms the youth's perception, leading them to see him as a mentor and source of valuable insights.
4.33	Symbolism, with the boat representing Alex's journey to bridge generational divides.	The construction of the boat symbolizes Alex's efforts to connect with the younger generation and pass on his knowledge and passion.
4.34	The value of intergenerational learning and the enduring relevance of life's experiences.	Alex's story explores the importance of sharing knowledge between generations, emphasizing the timeless value of experiential wisdom.
4.35	By showing how Alex's passion for the sea and sailing inspired and unified the community, particularly the youth.	The narrative highlights how individual interests, like Alex's love for sailing, can positively influence and bring together a community.
4.36	Her love for jazz and her desire to share its beauty with her community.	Mia's effort to introduce jazz to Melodiville is driven by her passion for the genre and her wish to share its enriching qualities.
4.37	Her passion and perseverance lead to a successful concert that changes the town's musical landscape.	Mia's character traits of determination and love for jazz culminate in a concert that transforms the community's musical preferences.
4.38	Imagery, describing the atmosphere of the park and the audience's reaction to the music.	The vivid imagery used to depict Mia's concert captures the emotional and communal impact of her jazz performance.
4.39	The impact of sharing one's passion and the importance of cultural diversity in art.	Mia's story highlights the value of exposing communities to diverse artistic expressions and the transformative power of personal passions.
4.40	By demonstrating that exposure to unfamiliar genres like jazz can enrich a community's cultural experience.	Mia's initiative to introduce jazz challenges Melodiville's musical norms, illustrating how diversity in art can broaden cultural appreciation.

ALEXANDER-GRACE EDUCATION

Topic 5 - Word Definitions

5.1) What is the definition of "abdicate"?

☐ Showing little concern for the feelings of others; harsh

☐ Accept or admit the existence or truth of

☐ A person who is addicted to a particular substance, typically an illegal drug

☐ To give up a position, right, or power

5.2) What is the definition of "abrasive"?

☐ Accept or admit the existence or truth of

☐ Showing little concern for the feelings of others; harsh

☐ Buy or obtain (an object) for oneself

☐ A person who is addicted to a particular substance, typically an illegal drug

5.3) What is the definition of "abruptly"?

☐ Make (someone) troubled or nervous

☐ A person who is addicted to a particular substance, typically an illegal drug

☐ Suddenly and unexpectedly

☐ Buy or obtain (an object) for oneself

5.4) What is the definition of "acknowledge"?

☐ Showing little concern for the feelings of others; harsh

☐ The state or process of affiliating or being affiliated

☐ Accept or admit the existence or truth of

☐ Warn or reprimand someone firmly

5.5) What is the definition of "acquire"?

☐ Accept or admit the existence or truth of

☐ Showing little concern for the feelings of others; harsh

☐ Make (someone) troubled or nervous

☐ Buy or obtain (an object) for oneself

5.6) What is the definition of "addict"?

☐ Suddenly and unexpectedly

☐ Satisfactory or acceptable in quality or quantity

☐ A person who is addicted to a particular substance, typically an illegal drug

☐ To give up a position, right, or power

5.7) What is the definition of "adequate"?

☐ A person who is addicted to a particular substance, typically an illegal drug

☐ Satisfactory or acceptable in quality or quantity

☐ Showing little concern for the feelings of others; harsh

☐ Warn or reprimand someone firmly

5.8) What is the definition of "admonish"?

☐ Suddenly and unexpectedly

☐ Buy or obtain (an object) for oneself

☐ Showing little concern for the feelings of others; harsh

☐ Warn or reprimand someone firmly

5.9) What is the definition of "affiliation"?

☐ Suddenly and unexpectedly

☐ Warn or reprimand someone firmly

☐ Showing little concern for the feelings of others; harsh

☐ The state or process of affiliating or being affiliated

5.10) What is the definition of "agitate"?

☐ Make (someone) troubled or nervous

☐ The state or process of affiliating or being affiliated

☐ Satisfactory or acceptable in quality or quantity

☐ A person who is addicted to a particular substance, typically an illegal drug

5.11) What is the definition of "connotation"?

☐ Accept or admit the existence or truth of

☐ Following continuously; in unbroken or logical sequence

☐ Described in, or as if in, a legend; famous

☐ An idea or feeling that a word invokes in addition to its literal or primary meaning

5.12) What is the definition of "legendary"?

☐ Make (someone) troubled or nervous

☐ Described in, or as if in, a legend; famous

☐ Required by law or rules; compulsory

☐ Warn or reprimand someone firmly

5.13) What is the definition of "consecutive"?

☐ An idea or feeling that a word invokes in addition to its literal or primary meaning

☐ Following continuously; in unbroken or logical sequence

☐ To give up a position, right, or power

☐ The state of being strikingly different from something else in juxtaposition or close association

5.14) What is the definition of "liaison"?

☐ Warn or reprimand someone firmly

☐ Following continuously; in unbroken or logical sequence

☐ Communication or cooperation that facilitates a close working relationship between people or organizations

☐ An idea or feeling that a word invokes in addition to its literal or primary meaning

5.15) What is the definition of "irrelevant"?

☐ Seek information or advice from (someone with expertise in a particular area)

☐ Showing little concern for the feelings of others; harsh

☐ Communication or cooperation that facilitates a close working relationship between people or organizations

☐ Not connected with or relevant to something

5.16) What is the definition of "libel"?

☐ A published false statement that is damaging to a person's reputation; a written defamation

☐ Accept or admit the existence or truth of

☐ The state of being strikingly different from something else in juxtaposition or close association

☐ Required by law or rules; compulsory

5.17) What is the definition of "consult"?

☐ A published false statement that is damaging to a person's reputation; a written defamation

☐ Following continuously; in unbroken or logical sequence

☐ Described in, or as if in, a legend; famous

☐ Seek information or advice from (someone with expertise in a particular area)

5.18) What is the definition of "ludicrous"?

☐ A person who is addicted to a particular substance, typically an illegal drug

☐ So foolish, unreasonable, or out of place as to be amusing; ridiculous

☐ Make (someone) troubled or nervous

☐ Communication or cooperation that facilitates a close working relationship between people or organizations

5.19) What is the definition of "contrast"?

☐ The state of being strikingly different from something else in juxtaposition or close association

☐ Make (someone) troubled or nervous

☐ Showing little concern for the feelings of others; harsh

☐ A published false statement that is damaging to a person's reputation; a written defamation

5.20) What is the definition of "mandatory"?

☐ An idea or feeling that a word invokes in addition to its literal or primary meaning

☐ A published false statement that is damaging to a person's reputation; a written defamation

☐ Required by law or rules; compulsory

☐ Showing little concern for the feelings of others; harsh

5.21) What is the definition of "fidget"?

□ A person who cannot stop doing or using something, especially something harmful

□ Following continuously; in unbroken or logical sequence

□ To make small movements, especially with no purpose

□ Communication or cooperation that facilitates a close working relationship between people or organizations

5.22) What is the definition of "copious"?

□ Required by law or rules; compulsory

□ Warn or reprimand someone firmly

□ A published false statement that is damaging to a person's reputation; a written defamation

□ Abundant in supply or quantity

5.23) What is the definition of "mitigate"?

□ Waste time; be slow

□ Make less severe, serious, or painful

□ So foolish, unreasonable, or out of place as to be amusing; ridiculous

□ Described in, or as if in, a legend; famous

5.24) What is the definition of "detrimental"?

□ Buy or obtain (an object) for oneself

□ Tending to cause harm

□ Enough, satisfactory or acceptable in quality or quantity

□ To have a close similarity; match or agree almost exactly

5.25) What is the definition of "correspond"?

☐ Showing little concern for the feelings of others; harsh

☐ To have a close similarity; match or agree almost exactly

☐ Make (someone) troubled or nervous

☐ Following continuously; in unbroken or logical sequence

5.26) What is the definition of "naive"?

☐ Warn or reprimand someone firmly

☐ Seek information or advice from (someone with expertise in a particular area)

☐ Showing a lack of experience, wisdom, or judgment

☐ Following continuously; in unbroken or logical sequence

5.27) What is the definition of "squander"?

☐ Warn or reprimand someone firmly

☐ Showing a lack of experience, wisdom, or judgment

☐ The state or process of affiliating or being affiliated

☐ To waste something, especially time or money

5.28) What is the definition of "dawdle"?

☐ Waste time; be slow

☐ To have a close similarity; match or agree almost exactly

☐ Enough, satisfactory or acceptable in quality or quantity

☐ Abundant in supply or quantity

5.29) What is the definition of "narrate"?

☐ Communication or cooperation that facilitates a close working relationship between people or organizations

☐ Warn or reprimand someone firmly

☐ Suddenly and unexpectedly

☐ Give a spoken or written account of

5.30) What is the definition of "dubbed"?

☐ Communication or cooperation that facilitates a close working relationship between people or organizations

☐ The state or process of affiliating or being affiliated

☐ Following continuously; in unbroken or logical sequence

☐ Give an unofficial name to something

5.31) What is the definition of "deceitful"?

☐ Make less severe, serious, or painful

☐ Intended to deceive; misleading; dishonest.

☐ The state or process of affiliating or being affiliated

☐ To disturb or excite emotionally; arouse; perturb.

5.32) What is the definition of "necessity"?

☐ Lazily careless; offhand.

☐ The fact of being required or indispensable.

☐ The state or process of affiliating or being affiliated

☐ Seek information or advice from (someone with expertise in a particular area)

5.33) What is the definition of "qualify"?

☐ Extremely unpleasant.

☐ To disturb or excite emotionally; arouse; perturb.

☐ Waste time; be slow

☐ To be entitled to a particular benefit

5.34) What is the definition of "demeanor"?

☐ Intended to deceive; misleading; dishonest.

☐ To disturb or excite emotionally; arouse; perturb.

☐ The state or process of affiliating or being affiliated

☐ Outward behavior; conduct.

5.35) What is the definition of "negligent"?

☐ Accept or admit the existence or truth of

☐ Lazily careless; offhand.

☐ Warn or reprimand someone firmly

☐ Showing a lack of experience, wisdom, or judgment

5.36) What is the definition of "allege"?

☐ A published false statement that is damaging to a person's reputation; a written defamation

☐ Lazily careless; offhand.

☐ To assert without proof.

☐ Buy or obtain (an object) for oneself

5.37) What is the definition of "derogatory"?

☐ To give up a position, right, or power

☐ Showing little concern for the feelings of others; harsh

☐ Buy or obtain (an object) for oneself

☐ Showing a critical or disrespectful attitude.

5.38) What is the definition of "obnoxious"?

☐ Give a spoken or written account of

☐ Buy or obtain (an object) for oneself

☐ Extremely unpleasant.

☐ The state or process of affiliating or being affiliated

5.39) What is the definition of "allocate"?

☐ Abundant in supply or quantity

☐ To disturb or excite emotionally; arouse; perturb.

☐ To distribute for a particular purpose.

☐ Communication or cooperation that facilitates a close working relationship between people or organizations

5.40) What is the definition of "devastate"?

☐ To destroy or ruin (something).

☐ Accept or admit the existence or truth of

☐ So foolish, unreasonable, or out of place as to be amusing; ridiculous

☐ To have a close similarity; match or agree almost exactly

ALEXANDER-GRACE EDUCATION

Topic 5 - Answers

Question Number	Answer	Explanation
5.1	To give up a position, right, or power	"Abdicate" means to formally give up a position of power or a right often that of a monarch or leader.
5.2	Showing little concern for the feelings of others; harsh	"Abrasive" describes a personality or approach that is harsh and insensitive, often causing upset or irritation.
5.3	Suddenly and unexpectedly	"Abruptly" refers to something happening quickly and without warning, catching people off guard.
5.4	Accept or admit the existence or truth of	"Acknowledge" involves recognizing or admitting the truth or existence of something.
5.5	Buy or obtain (an object) for oneself	"Acquire" means to come into possession of something, often through buying or receiving it.
5.6	A person who is addicted to a particular substance, typically an illegal drug	"Addict" refers to someone who cannot stop using a substance, showing a dependency on it.
5.7	Satisfactory or acceptable in quality or quantity	"Adequate" means enough or satisfactory for a particular purpose, meeting the necessary requirements.
5.8	Warn or reprimand someone firmly	"Admonish" is to caution or advise someone against something, often in a warning or reprimanding manner.
5.9	The state or process of affiliating or being affiliated	"Affiliation" refers to the connection or association with a group or organization, often for mutual benefit.
5.10	Make (someone) troubled or nervous	"Agitate" means to disturb or upset someone, causing them to feel anxious or nervous.
5.11	An idea or feeling that a word invokes in addition to its literal or primary meaning	"Connotation" refers to the associated or secondary meaning of a word, beyond its direct definition.
5.12	Described in, or as if in, a legend; famous	"Legendary" applies to something or someone very famous or well-known, often because of exceptional qualities.
5.13	Following continuously; in unbroken or logical sequence	"Consecutive" means one after the other without interruption, in a continuous and sequential manner.
5.14	Communication or cooperation that facilitates a close working relationship between people or organizations	"Liaison" denotes a form of communication or cooperation which helps to establish a partnership or relationship.
5.15	Not connected with or relevant to something	"Irrelevant" describes something that does not relate to the current topic or situation, lacking significance.
5.16	A published false statement that is damaging to a person's reputation; a written defamation	"Libel" involves making false statements in written form that harm someone's reputation.
5.17	Seek information or advice from (someone with expertise in a particular area)	"Consult" means to ask for advice or information from someone, especially an expert or professional.
5.18	So foolish, unreasonable, or out of place as to be amusing; ridiculous	"Ludicrous" describes something that is so absurd or unreasonable that it becomes funny.

5.19	The state of being strikingly different from something else in juxtaposition or close association	"Contrast" refers to the difference that is clearly visible when comparing two or more things.
5.20	Required by law or rules; compulsory	"Mandatory" means something that is obligatory or required, often by law or regulation.
5.21	To make small movements, especially with no purpose	"Fidget" describes the act of making small movements, often as a way to relieve nervousness or boredom.
5.22	Abundant in supply or quantity	"Copious" means available in large quantities; plentiful or abundant.
5.23	Make less severe, serious, or painful	"Mitigate" involves reducing the severity, harshness, or pain of something.
5.24	Tending to cause harm	"Detrimental" means causing damage or harm, often in a way that is not immediately obvious.
5.25	To have a close similarity; match or agree almost exactly	"Correspond" means to have a similarity or be equivalent in some way, often in characteristics or function.
5.26	Showing a lack of experience, wisdom, or judgment	"Naive" describes someone who lacks experience, wisdom, or judgment, often being overly trusting or simple.
5.27	To waste something, especially time or money	"Squander" means to use something valuable in a wasteful or pointless manner, not utilizing it properly.
5.28	Waste time; be slow	"Dawdle" means to waste time or be slow in movement or action, often procrastinating.
5.29	Give a spoken or written account of	"Narrate" involves telling a story or giving an account of events, either orally or in writing.
5.30	Give an unofficial name to something	"Dubbed" means to give someone or something a nickname or title, often informally.
5.31	Intended to deceive; misleading; dishonest.	"Deceitful" describes behavior or actions intended to deceive or mislead others.
5.32	The fact of being required or indispensable.	"Necessity" refers to something that is essential or needed, often for a particular purpose or situation.
5.33	To be entitled to a particular benefit	"Qualify" means to meet the necessary conditions to be eligible for something, such as a competition or benefit.
5.34	Outward behavior; conduct.	"Demeanor" refers to the outward behavior or bearing of a person, indicating their character or mood.
5.35	Lazily careless; offhand.	"Negligent" describes a lack of proper care or attention, often resulting in harm or mistakes.
5.36	To assert without proof.	"Allege" means to claim that something is true without providing evidence, often in legal or formal contexts.
5.37	Showing a critical or disrespectful attitude.	"Derogatory" refers to comments or attitudes that are disrespectful or critical in a demeaning way.
5.38	Extremely unpleasant.	"Obnoxious" describes something or someone that is extremely unpleasant or annoying.
5.39	To distribute for a particular purpose.	"Allocate" involves setting something aside for a specific purpose or to distribute resources in a planned way.
5.40	To destroy or ruin (something).	"Devastate" means to cause great destruction or damage, often leaving ruin in its wake.

Topic 6 - Reading Comprehension

While exploring the attic of his new home, Marcus found a mysterious chest filled with old books and maps. Among them was a diary belonging to an adventurer who had traveled the world. Fascinated, Marcus spent days reading the diary, living through the adventures and discovering places he had never heard of. The stories of friendship, bravery, and exploration inspired Marcus to plan his own adventure, starting with a map he found in the chest that hinted at a hidden treasure in his own town.

6.1) What initially captures Marcus's interest in the attic?

☐ A family photo album

☐ A model airplane

☐ A mysterious chest

☐ A ghost

6.2) What does Marcus find in the chest?

☐ Jewelry

☐ A map to a hidden treasure

☐ A diary belonging to an adventurer

☐ Old toys

6.3) How does Marcus feel about reading the adventurer's diary?

☐ Scared

☐ Confused

☐ Inspired

☐ Bored

6.4) What theme is most prominent in the story?

☐ Loneliness

☐ Overcoming adversity

☐ Fear of the unknown

☐ Joy of discovery

6.5) What does Marcus plan to do after reading the diary?

☐ Ignore the maps

☐ Plan his own adventure

☐ Sell the chest

☐ Write his own diary

Eva, a curious and adventurous girl, stumbled upon a hidden cave near her home one summer afternoon. Inside, she found walls covered in ancient paintings that told stories of a civilization long gone. With each step deeper into the cave, she discovered artifacts and symbols that sparked her imagination. Eva realized she had uncovered a secret passage to understanding the past. Filled with excitement, she decided to document her findings and share them with her classmates, hoping to inspire them with the same sense of wonder and adventure.

6.6) What initially leads Eva to the hidden cave?

☐ A map

☐ A friend's suggestion

☐ Her curiosity and adventurous spirit

☐ An accident

6.7) What does Eva find inside the cave?

☐ Gold and jewels

☐ Ancient paintings and artifacts

☐ Modern technology

☐ A lost animal

6.8) What does the story suggest about Eva's personality?

☐ She is curious and adventurous

☐ She dislikes history

☐ She is uninterested in exploration

☐ She is timid

6.9) How does Eva plan to share her discovery?

☐ By selling the artifacts

☐ By documenting and sharing with her classmates

☐ By forgetting about it

☐ By keeping it a secret

6.10) What is the main theme of the new story?

☐ The value of wealth

☐ The importance of staying home

☐ The dangers of exploration

☐ The thrill of discovery and sharing knowledge

On a windy afternoon, Alex and Sam discovered an old, rusted key while playing in the park. Curious about its origin, they embarked on a quest to find what it unlocked. Their adventure led them to an ancient library at the edge of town. Inside, they found a secret door that the key opened, revealing a room full of old books and maps of the world. With each book they read, Alex and Sam learned about legends, myths, and history they never knew existed, sparking a lifelong love for learning and exploration.

6.11) What triggers Alex and Sam's adventure?

☐ Finding an old, rusted key

☐ A story told by their grandparents

☐ A dream about a hidden treasure

☐ A map they found at home

6.12) Where does their quest lead them?

☐ To a secret beach

☐ To a mysterious castle

☐ To an ancient library

☐ To a hidden cave

6.13) What do Alex and Sam discover in the library?

☐ A hidden passage to another dimension

☐ A secret door opened by the key

☐ A treasure chest

☐ A ghost

6.14) How does the discovery in the library affect them?

☐ They become scared of adventures

☐ It sparks a lifelong love for learning

☐ They lose interest in exploration

☐ They decide to become librarians

6.15) What is the main theme of the third story?

☐ The dangers of curiosity

☐ The value of friendship and adventure

☐ The joy of finding lost items

☐ The importance of preserving history

In a small coastal town, Leah discovered an old lighthouse that was said to be haunted. Driven by her love for mysteries, she decided to investigate it one evening. As she explored the lighthouse, she encountered various clues that hinted at its past as a haven for lost sailors. Leah realized the so-called hauntings were just stories passed down through generations, masking the true history of the lighthouse as a beacon of hope. Inspired by her findings, Leah organized a community project to restore the lighthouse and celebrate its real story.

6.16) What motivates Leah to investigate the old lighthouse?

☐ A dare from friends

☐ A school assignment

☐ Her interest in architecture

☐ Her love for mysteries

6.17) What does Leah find out about the lighthouse?

□ It was abandoned due to a curse

□ It contained hidden treasure

□ It was a haven for lost sailors

□ It was actually haunted

6.18) How does Leah's perception of the lighthouse change?

□ She appreciates its true history

□ She loses interest in it

□ She wants to sell the story to a magazine

□ She becomes afraid of it

6.19) What action does Leah take after her investigation?

□ She writes a book about it

□ She sells the lighthouse

□ She avoids the lighthouse

□ She organizes a community project to restore it

6.20) What is the main theme of the fourth story?

□ Unraveling mysteries and appreciating history

□ The supernatural

□ Overcoming fear

□ The power of community

Nora and her grandfather, a retired sea captain, discovered an old maritime map among his belongings. The map depicted an uncharted island said to be the resting place of a legendary shipwreck. Together, they decided to embark on an expedition to find the island. Their journey was filled with challenges, but Nora's resolve and her grandfather's experience at sea guided them through. Upon finding the island, they uncovered not only the wreck but also a story of bravery and perseverance that had been lost to the sea. This adventure brought Nora and her grandfather closer, teaching Nora the value of courage and family legacy.

6.21) What prompts Nora and her grandfather to start their expedition?

☐ A message in a bottle

☐ A dream about the sea

☐ An old maritime map

☐ A family legend

6.22) What do they hope to find on the uncharted island?

☐ A new species of plant

☐ Buried treasure

☐ A legendary shipwreck

☐ A lost civilization

6.23) What is a major theme of their adventure?

☐ Magic and mysticism

☐ Betrayal and revenge

☐ Romance and relationships

☐ Bravery and perseverance

6.24) How does the journey affect Nora and her grandfather's relationship?

☐ It doesn't change anything

☐ They become competitive with each other

☐ It causes a rift between them

☐ It brings them closer together

6.25) What lesson does Nora learn from the expedition?

☐ The dangers of the unknown

☐ The importance of being prepared

☐ The benefits of wealth

☐ The value of courage and family legacy

During a summer camp in the dense forest, Mia and her friends stumbled upon an ancient stone tablet with inscriptions. Intrigued by its mysterious symbols, they took it to their camp leader, who was a history enthusiast. Together, they deciphered the inscriptions, which told of a guardian spirit that protected the forest and its inhabitants. The story inspired Mia and her friends to explore the forest more respectfully, understanding its significance and the balance between nature and its guardians. Their adventure led them to appreciate the legends and the natural world around them, fostering a sense of responsibility towards conserving it for future generations.

6.26) What do Mia and her friends find in the forest?

☐ A hidden treasure

☐ A lost city

☐ A rare animal species

☐ An ancient stone tablet

6.27) Who helps them decipher the inscriptions on the tablet?

☐ A mysterious stranger

☐ A local historian

☐ A forest ranger

☐ Their camp leader

6.28) What is revealed by the inscriptions?

☐ A curse on the forest

☐ The location of hidden gold

☐ Directions to a secret waterfall

☐ A story of a guardian spirit

6.29) How does the discovery affect their perception of the forest?

☐ They gain a deeper respect for it

☐ They start a fire to signal for help

☐ They become fearful of it

☐ They decide to leave the camp

6.30) What lesson do Mia and her friends learn from their adventure?

☐ How to survive in the wild

☐ The importance of teamwork

☐ The thrill of discovery

☐ The value of respecting nature

During a school trip to a historic castle, Zack found a secret chamber hidden behind a tapestry. Inside, there was a collection of ancient artifacts and a large, dusty book filled with tales of knights and their noble deeds. Zack was captivated by one story in particular, about a knight who protected the castle and its lands with wisdom and bravery. Sharing the discovery with his friends, Zack inspired them to act out the stories, deepening their appreciation for history and the lessons it offers. The trip became an unforgettable adventure, turning history into a living, breathing experience for Zack and his classmates.

6.31) Where does Zack find the secret chamber?

□ Underneath a bridge

□ Inside a haunted house

□ In his school

□ Behind a tapestry in a historic castle

6.32) What captivates Zack in the chamber?

□ A set of ancient armor

□ A dusty book of knight tales

□ A mysterious potion

□ A hidden treasure

6.33) What theme is explored through the knight's story?

□ Trickery and deceit

□ Magic and mystery

□ Love and betrayal

□ Wisdom and bravery

6.34) How do Zack and his friends use the discovery?

☐ They report it to their teacher

☐ They ignore it

☐ They sell the artifacts

☐ They act out the stories

6.35) What impact does the trip have on Zack and his classmates?

☐ It scares them away from history

☐ It bores them

☐ It confuses them

☐ It makes history come alive for them

Ava, a young artist, moved to a new town and felt lost among its unfamiliar streets and faces. Seeking inspiration, she wandered into a quiet park, where she found a statue of a woman, labeled 'The Town's Founder'. Intrigued, Ava began researching the founder's life and discovered she was also an artist who had overcome great obstacles to build the community. Motivated by the founder's story, Ava decided to create a series of paintings that captured the spirit of the town and its people. Her art exhibition became a bridge between her and the town, making her feel at home and inspiring others to pursue their passions.

6.36) What initially makes Ava feel lost in the new town?

☐ The unfriendly people

☐ The cold weather

☐ The lack of art

☐ The unfamiliar streets and faces

6.37) What sparks Ava's interest in the park?

☐ A lost kitten

☐ A statue of the town's founder

☐ A group of musicians

☐ A beautiful garden

6.38) What is significant about the town's founder?

☐ She was an artist and community builder

☐ She discovered gold

☐ She was a wealthy merchant

☐ She was a famous actress

6.39) How does Ava decide to connect with the town?

☐ By writing a book

☐ By starting a new business

☐ By creating a series of paintings

☐ By leaving the town

6.40) What theme is explored through Ava's actions?

☐ The challenge of moving to a new place

☐ The power of art to connect people

☐ The difficulties of being a young artist

☐ The importance of historical research

ALEXANDER-GRACE EDUCATION

Topic 6 - Answers

Question Number	Answer	Explanation
6.1	A mysterious chest	Marcus's interest is piqued by finding a mysterious chest in the attic, indicating his curiosity and sense of adventure.
6.2	A diary belonging to an adventurer	Inside the chest, Marcus finds a diary that belonged to an adventurer, sparking his interest in exploration.
6.3	Inspired	Reading the adventurer's diary inspires Marcus, motivating him to explore and embark on his own adventures.
6.4	Joy of discovery	The theme of joy of discovery is most prominent as Marcus explores new places and plans his adventure.
6.5	Plan his own adventure	After reading the diary, Marcus is motivated to plan his own adventure, indicating his inspired state of mind.
6.6	Her curiosity and adventurous spirit	Eva's curiosity and adventurous spirit lead her to discover the hidden cave, highlighting her explorative nature.
6.7	Ancient paintings and artifacts	Inside the cave, Eva finds ancient paintings and artifacts, revealing the cave's historical significance.
6.8	She is curious and adventurous	Eva's personality is shown to be curious and adventurous, driving her to explore and make discoveries.
6.9	By documenting and sharing with her classmates	Eva plans to document her findings and share them with her classmates, spreading her sense of wonder.
6.10	The thrill of discovery and sharing knowledge	The main theme is the thrill of discovery and the importance of sharing that knowledge with others.
6.11	Finding an old, rusted key	Alex and Sam's adventure begins when they find an old, rusted key, sparking their curiosity.
6.12	To an ancient library	Their quest leads them to an ancient library, where they hope to uncover the key's purpose.
6.13	A secret door opened by the key	In the library, they discover a secret door that the key opens, revealing a room full of old books and maps.
6.14	It sparks a lifelong love for learning	The discovery ignites a lifelong love for learning and exploration in both Alex and Sam.
6.15	The value of friendship and adventure	The main theme is the value of friendship and the enriching nature of adventure and learning.
6.16	Her love for mysteries	Leah's investigation of the lighthouse is driven by her love for mysteries, showing her inquisitive nature.
6.17	It was a haven for lost sailors	Leah finds out that the lighthouse served as a haven for lost sailors, debunking the haunted stories.
6.18	She appreciates its true history	Leah's perception changes as she appreciates the lighthouse's true history as a beacon of hope.

5.19	She organizes a community project to restore it	Leah takes action by organizing a project to restore the lighthouse, showing her initiative and leadership.
5.20	Unraveling mysteries and appreciating history	The main theme is unraveling mysteries and appreciating the true history and significance of places.
5.21	An old maritime map	Nora and her grandfather are inspired to start their expedition by discovering an old maritime map.
5.22	A legendary shipwreck	They hope to find a legendary shipwreck on the uncharted island, driven by the map's clues.
5.23	Bravery and perseverance	Their adventure emphasizes the themes of bravery and perseverance in the face of challenges.
5.24	It brings them closer together	The journey strengthens their relationship, bringing Nora and her grandfather closer together.
5.25	The value of courage and family legacy	Nora learns the importance of courage and the value of family legacy, inspired by their successful expedition.
5.26	An ancient stone tablet	Mia and her friends find an ancient stone tablet in the forest, sparking their interest in its origins.
5.27	Their camp leader	The camp leader helps them decipher the tablet's inscriptions, utilizing his history expertise.
5.28	A story of a guardian spirit	The inscriptions reveal a story about a guardian spirit protecting the forest, intriguing the group.
5.29	They gain a deeper respect for it	The discovery leads them to respect the forest more, understanding its significance and the balance with nature.
5.30	The value of respecting nature	The adventure teaches Mia and her friends the importance of respecting and conserving nature.
5.31	Behind a tapestry in a historic castle	Zack finds the secret chamber hidden behind a tapestry in a castle, marking the start of their adventure.
5.32	A dusty book of knight tales	Zack is captivated by a book filled with tales of knights, inspiring him and his friends to learn more.
5.33	Wisdom and bravery	The knight's story explores themes of wisdom and bravery, resonating with Zack and his friends.
5.34	They act out the stories	They use the discovery to act out the stories, bringing history to life and deepening their appreciation for it.
5.35	It makes history come alive for them	The trip transforms history into a vivid and engaging experience for Zack and his classmates.
5.36	The unfamiliar streets and faces	Ava feels lost due to the new and unfamiliar surroundings in the town, seeking a sense of belonging.
5.37	A statue of the town's founder	A statue in the park piques Ava's interest, leading her to explore the founder's life and impact.
5.38	She was an artist and community builder	The town's founder was also an artist who overcame obstacles to build the community, inspiring Ava.
5.39	By creating a series of paintings	Ava decides to connect with the town by creating paintings that capture its spirit, using her art to bridge gaps.
5.40	The power of art to connect people	Ava's story explores the power of art to connect people, inspire passion, and foster a sense of community.

Topic 7 – Evaluating Author's Craft

In the small coastal town of Sea Breeze, young Lily discovered an old diary in her grandmother's attic. The diary, dating back a century, belonged to a mysterious figure known as 'The Sea Whisperer.' Intrigued, Lily spent evenings reading, uncovering stories of sea adventures, hidden treasures, and age-old legends. One tale, in particular, spoke of a hidden cove that held a secret of the town's past. Driven by curiosity, Lily embarked on a quest, finding that reality and legend were intricately woven, leading to a discovery that would change her understanding of the town's history.

7.1) How does the author use imagery in the story about Lily?

☐ By focusing on the diary's physical appearance

☐ By vividly describing the sea adventures

☐ By using complex metaphors

☐ By detailing Lily's daily routine

7.2) What literary technique is used to introduce the Sea Whisperer?

☐ Foreshadowing

☐ Flashback

☐ Symbolism

☐ Allegory

7.3) What effect does the diary have on the progression of the story?

☐ It confuses the main character

☐ It adds unnecessary details

☐ It serves as a key to unlocking the town's history

☐ It slows down the plot

7.4) How does the author build suspense around the hidden cove?

☐ Through hints and mysterious tales

☐ By revealing its location early on

☐ By making it the story's primary setting

☐ Through detailed historical facts

7.5) What theme is most evident in Lily's quest?

☐ The danger of the sea

☐ The simplicity of small-town life

☐ The importance of family

☐ The thrill of discovery

In the bustling city of Metroville, a hidden alleyway led to an extraordinary little bookshop, known only to a few. 12-year-old Max, an inquisitive and book-loving boy, stumbled upon it while chasing his runaway dog, Buster. The bookshop, run by an eccentric old man, was filled with books that seemed to come alive with stories. One book, in particular, caught Max's attention: a tale about a secret garden with magical powers. As Max read, he noticed peculiar parallels between the story and his own life, leading him to wonder if the book was more than just fiction. This discovery ignited a passion for reading in Max, who began to see the magic in the everyday world.

7.6) How does the author use imagery to describe the bookshop?

☐ As a dark and scary location

☐ As an extraordinary and magical place

☐ As a modern and sleek store

☐ As an ordinary and unremarkable place

ALEXANDER-GRACE EDUCATION

7.7) What literary technique is used to show the connection between the book's story and Max's life?

☐ Irony

☐ Metaphor

☐ Parallel plot

☐ Hyperbole

7.8) What theme is explored through Max's discovery in the bookshop?

☐ The importance of caring for pets

☐ The challenge of urban living

☐ The joy of finding hidden places

☐ The excitement of magical adventures

7.9) Which narrative technique adds a sense of mystery to the bookshop?

☐ Flashback to Max's childhood

☐ Detailed descriptions of the books

☐ Foreshadowing of future events

☐ A sudden twist in the plot

7.10) How does Max's perception of the world change after his experience?

☐ He becomes fearful of the unknown

☐ He sees magic in the everyday world

☐ He loses interest in books

☐ He becomes more skeptical

In the small village of Pinegrove, nestled in the mountains, an annual storytelling festival brought the community together. Sarah, a young girl with a talent for writing, decided to participate for the first time. Her story, set in a mystical forest, used vivid imagery to bring characters to life and foreshadowed events through subtle hints in dialogue and descriptions. As she narrated, the audience was captivated by the magical world she created, feeling the emotions of the characters. Sarah's story, rich with flashbacks revealing the forest's ancient secrets, not only won the festival but also inspired her peers to see the power of storytelling in shaping perspectives and emotions.

7.11) How does Sarah use imagery in her story?

☐ To create a realistic setting

☐ To bring the mystical forest to life

☐ To detail her writing process

☐ To describe the festival

'

7.12) What narrative technique does Sarah use to add depth to her story?

☐ Focusing on a single character

☐ Flashbacks revealing ancient secrets

☐ Presenting the story in chronological order

☐ Using only dialogue

7.13) How does Sarah foreshadow events in her story?

☐ Using subtle hints in dialogue and descriptions

☐ By directly stating future events

☐ Through the characters' dreams

☐ With a narrator explaining the plot

7.14) What effect does Sarah's story have on the audience?

☐ It confuses them

☐ It makes them sleepy

☐ It leads them to leave the festival

☐ It captivates them with the magical world

7.15) What theme is evident in Sarah's storytelling approach?

☐ The importance of winning competitions

☐ The challenges of writing

☐ The power of storytelling in shaping perspectives

☐ The simplicity of village life

In the bustling city, an old clock tower stood as a silent witness to centuries of change. Lucas, a teenage history buff, was drawn to its timeless presence. One night, he discovered a hidden compartment in the tower revealing old letters and photographs. These artifacts told stories of people and events connected to the clock tower. Through flashbacks in his imagination, Lucas saw the tower's role in the city's history, from joyful celebrations to somber moments. The letters painted vivid imagery of life in different eras, allowing Lucas to connect the past with the present. His experience at the tower inspired him to write a historical narrative, blending fact and fiction to bring the clock tower's legacy to life.

7.16) What technique does the author use to describe the clock tower's history?

☐ Symbolism

☐ Personification

☐ Flashbacks

☐ Metaphor

7.17) How does Lucas's discovery in the tower influence the narrative?

□ It shifts the setting to another city

□ It adds mystery to the story

□ It creates a historical context

□ It introduces a new character

7.18) What effect do the old letters and photographs have on the story?

□ They change the genre of the story

□ They confuse the main character

□ They provide vivid imagery of different eras

□ They lead to a futuristic twist

7.19) How does Lucas use his experience at the tower?

□ To renovate the tower

□ To sell the artifacts

□ To abandon his interest in history

□ To write a historical narrative

7.20) What theme is most evident through Lucas's exploration of the clock tower?

□ The thrill of urban exploration

□ The connection between past and present

□ The danger of old buildings

□ The fear of change

In the small town of Maplewood, an old legend spoke of a hidden waterfall that could only be seen under the full moon. Julia, a creative and adventurous girl, was captivated by this legend. One full moon night, she ventured into the forest, guided by the moonlight and the faint sound of water. Along her journey, Julia encountered mysterious symbols and enigmatic creatures that seemed to come straight out of a fairytale. As she finally found the waterfall, she realized that it was not just a natural wonder but a symbol of the magical world hidden within the ordinary. This revelation inspired her to write a series of stories, using rich imagery and foreshadowing to bring the mystical elements of Maplewood to life.

7.21) What literary technique does the author use to depict the hidden waterfall?

□ Sarcasm

□ Symbolism

□ Hyperbole

□ Allegory

7.22) How does Julia's adventure enhance the story's magical theme?

□ By using technical language

□ By focusing on daily life in Maplewood

□ By using realistic descriptions

□ By introducing enigmatic creatures

7.23) What effect is created by the imagery of the moonlit forest and waterfall?

□ An atmosphere of sadness

□ A mood of excitement and chaos

□ A feeling of wonder and magic

□ A sense of fear and danger

7.24) How does foreshadowing contribute to the story's plot?

☐ By hinting at the magical world within the ordinary

☐ By revealing the ending at the beginning

☐ By predicting future events in Maplewood

☐ By describing unrelated events

7.25) What theme does Julia's revelation at the waterfall reflect?

☐ The thrill of urban exploration

☐ The importance of following rules

☐ The danger of exploring alone at night

☐ The magic hidden in everyday life

In the heart of the bustling city, a mysterious mural appeared overnight on a blank wall. The mural, painted in vibrant colors, depicted a phoenix rising from the ashes. Mia, an art student with a keen eye for detail, was captivated by its beauty and hidden meanings. She started investigating the mural's origin, discovering that it was created by an anonymous artist known for their thought-provoking work. As Mia delved deeper, she uncovered stories interwoven into the mural's imagery, each representing themes of resilience, renewal, and hope. This journey of discovery led Mia to appreciate the power of art in conveying deep messages, inspiring her to create her own artwork that reflected her journey through the city's soul.

7.26) What technique does the artist use in the mural to symbolize transformation?

☐ Personification

☐ Metaphor

☐ Alliteration

☐ Simile

7.27) How does the mural's imagery influence Mia's perception of the city?

☐ It reveals the city's hidden beauty and depth

☐ It makes her fear the city

☐ It confuses her

☐ It has no effect on her perception

7.28) What theme is most prominent in the mural's depiction of the phoenix?

☐ Fear of change

☐ Resilience and hope

☐ Loneliness and isolation

☐ Joy of discovery

7.29) How does Mia's investigation into the mural enhance the story?

☐ It introduces a new character

☐ It leads to a scientific discovery

☐ It shifts the focus to a historical context

☐ It creates a sense of mystery

7.30) What impact does the mural have on Mia's artistic journey?

☐ It inspires her to create artwork reflecting her journey

☐ It discourages her from creating art

☐ It leads her to abandon art

☐ It makes her copy the mural's style

In the quiet town of Elmridge, a centuries-old tree stood in the center of the main square, known as the 'Wisdom Tree.' Jake, a thoughtful teenager with a love for folklore, often spent time under the tree, reading and daydreaming. One day, he found a carved inscription on the tree that read, 'Seek and ye shall find.' This message led Jake on a quest to uncover the hidden history of Elmridge. Through his journey, he encountered tales of the tree's significance in key events, each story told through flashbacks. The Wisdom Tree was not just a landmark; it was a storyteller, sharing lessons of wisdom, courage, and unity. Jake's discovery inspired him to write a historical piece for the town's newspaper, bringing the community together through shared heritage.

7.31) What role does the 'Wisdom Tree' play in the story?

☐ An obstacle for the main character

☐ A key character revealing the town's history

☐ A symbol of nature's beauty

☐ A mere backdrop

7.32) How does the author use flashbacks in the narrative?

☐ To confuse the reader

☐ To describe Jake's childhood

☐ To highlight modern technology

☐ To tell stories of the tree's past

7.33) What does the inscription 'Seek and ye shall find' foreshadow?

☐ An upcoming storm

☐ A romantic subplot

☐ A treasure hunt

☐ Jake's quest to uncover history

ALEXANDER-GRACE EDUCATION

7.34) What effect does Jake's historical piece have on the community?

☐ It leads to the tree being cut down

☐ It causes controversy

☐ It is largely ignored

☐ It brings the community together

7.35) What theme is most prominent in Jake's story?

☐ The value of heritage and shared stories

☐ The impact of technology

☐ The thrill of adventure

☐ The danger of urban development

In the futuristic city of New Eden, a peculiar sculpture stood in the central plaza, changing shapes with the passing hours. Kai, a tech-savvy teenager with a flair for art, was intrigued by its ever-evolving form. He learned that the sculpture was an interactive art piece, responding to the emotions and movements of the people around it. Fascinated, Kai spent days observing and documenting the sculpture's transformations, discovering it was a visual representation of the city's collective mood. As Kai delved into the art and science behind the sculpture, he uncovered stories of innovation, collaboration, and the human connection to technology. His exploration led to a deeper understanding of New Eden, inspiring him to create a digital art project that mirrored the dynamic nature of the sculpture and the city itself.

7.36) What narrative technique does the author use to describe the sculpture in New Eden?

☐ Allegory

☐ Imagery

☐ Simile

☐ Satire

7.37) How does Kai's interaction with the sculpture influence the plot?

□ It has no significant impact

□ It causes the sculpture to malfunction

□ It introduces a conflict

□ It leads to a deeper understanding of the city

7.38) What theme is explored through the sculpture's changing forms?

□ The permanence of art

□ The unpredictability of nature

□ The dynamic nature of human emotions

□ The simplicity of modern life

7.39) What effect is created by the sculpture responding to people's emotions and movements?

□ A sense of confusion

□ A feeling of alienation

□ A mood of sadness

□ An atmosphere of interactivity and connection

7.40) How does Kai's digital art project reflect his experience?

□ It imitates traditional art forms

□ It depicts futuristic technology

□ It mirrors the dynamic nature of the sculpture and city

□ It focuses on historical events

Topic 7 – Answers

Question Number	Answer	Explanation
7.1	By vividly describing the sea adventures	The author uses imagery to bring to life the sea adventures described in the diary, creating vivid mental pictures for the reader.
7.2	Symbolism	The Sea Whisperer is introduced as a symbolic figure representing mystery and adventure.
7.3	It serves as a key to unlocking the town's history	The diary plays a crucial role in advancing the plot by revealing the town's past and leading to Lily's quest.
7.4	Through hints and mysterious tales	The author builds suspense around the hidden cove through mysterious tales and subtle hints.
7.5	The thrill of discovery	Lily's quest is driven by the thrill of discovering the town's secrets and her own sense of adventure.
7.6	As an extraordinary and magical place	The bookshop is described using imagery that portrays it as a magical and extraordinary place, sparking Max's curiosity.
7.7	Parallel plot	The parallel plot technique shows the connection between the book's story and Max's life, adding depth to the narrative.
7.8	The joy of finding hidden places	The theme of discovering hidden gems in everyday life, like the magical bookshop, is explored in the story.
7.9	A sudden twist in the plot	The sudden discovery of the bookshop adds a sense of mystery and unexpectedness to the narrative.
7.10	He sees magic in the everyday world	After his experience, Max's perception of the world changes, and he begins to see magic in everyday life.
7.11	To bring the mystical forest to life	Sarah uses vivid imagery to bring the mystical forest and its characters to life in her story.
7.12	Flashbacks revealing ancient secrets	Sarah uses flashbacks to reveal the ancient secrets of the forest, adding depth and history to her story.
7.13	Using subtle hints in dialogue and descriptions	Sarah foreshadows events in her story by incorporating subtle hints in the dialogue and descriptions.
7.14	It captivates them with the magical world	The audience is captivated by the magical world Sarah creates, indicating the effectiveness of her storytelling.
7.15	The power of storytelling in shaping perspectives	Sarah's story highlights the power of storytelling to shape perspectives and emotions.
7.16	Flashbacks	The author uses flashbacks to narrate the clock tower's history through Lucas's imagination.
7.17	It creates a historical context	Lucas's discovery in the tower provides a historical context to the story, enriching the narrative.
7.18	They provide vivid imagery of different eras	The letters and photographs offer vivid imagery, allowing Lucas to visualize life in different eras.

7.19	To write a historical narrative	Lucas uses his experience at the tower to write a historical narrative, blending fact and fiction.
7.20	The connection between past and present	The story revolves around the theme of connecting the past with the present through the clock tower's history.
7.21	Symbolism	The author uses symbolism to depict the hidden waterfall as a magical and elusive element of the natural world.
7.22	By introducing enigmatic creatures	Julia's adventure is enhanced by the introduction of mysterious creatures, emphasizing the magical theme of the story.
7.23	A feeling of wonder and magic	The imagery of the moonlit forest and waterfall creates an atmosphere of wonder and magic.
7.24	By hinting at the magical world within the ordinary	Foreshadowing in the story hints at the magical world hidden in everyday life, adding depth to the plot.
7.25	The magic hidden in everyday life	Julia's revelation at the waterfall reflects the theme of finding magic and wonder in the everyday world.
7.26	Metaphor	The metaphor of the phoenix rising from the ashes is used to symbolize transformation and renewal in the mural.
7.27	It reveals the city's hidden beauty and depth	The mural influences Mia's perception by revealing the city's hidden beauty and depth through its art.
7.28	Resilience and hope	The mural's depiction of the phoenix rising from the ashes explores themes of resilience and hope.
7.29	It creates a sense of mystery	Mia's investigation into the mural's origin adds a sense of mystery and intrigue to the story.
7.30	It inspires her to create artwork reflecting her journey	Mia's experience with the mural inspires her to create her own artwork that reflects her journey through the city.
7.31	A key character revealing the town's history	The 'Wisdom Tree' plays a crucial role in the story as a character that reveals the town's history to Jake.
7.32	To tell stories of the tree's past	The author uses flashbacks to tell stories of the tree's past, adding depth to the narrative.
7.33	Jake's quest to uncover history	The inscription foreshadows Jake's quest to uncover the hidden history of Elmridge.
7.34	It brings the community together	Jake's historical piece about the Wisdom Tree brings the community together, emphasizing shared heritage.
7.35	The value of heritage and shared stories	Jake's story highlights the importance of heritage and shared stories, emphasizing their impact on the community.
7.36	Imagery	The author uses imagery to describe the ever-changing sculpture in New Eden, emphasizing its dynamic nature.
7.37	It leads to a deeper understanding of the city	Kai's interaction with the sculpture influences the plot by leading to a deeper understanding of the city and its people.
7.38	The dynamic nature of human emotions	The theme of human emotions' dynamic nature is explored through the sculpture's changing forms in response to people.
7.39	An atmosphere of interactivity and connection	The sculpture's responsiveness creates an atmosphere of interactivity and connection between art and the city's inhabitants.
7.40	It mirrors the dynamic nature of the sculpture and city	Kai's digital art project reflects his experience with the sculpture, mirroring the dynamic nature of both the art and the city.

Topic 8 – Critical Analysis of Texts

In the small town of Greenfield, a debate arose about whether to build a new community park. The local newspaper published articles with differing viewpoints. One article argued that the park would provide a much-needed recreational space for families and improve community health. Another article suggested that the town's budget would be better spent on improving schools. Maya, a seventh-grader, was assigned to write a report summarizing these articles and presenting her own opinion. As she researched and analyzed the articles, Maya learned to identify the authors' biases and assumptions, and how to evaluate their arguments based on evidence.

8.1) How does the first article attempt to persuade readers about the park?

☐ By showing the financial impact

☐ By comparing it to other towns' projects

☐ By using negative language about the town

☐ By emphasizing health and recreational benefits

8.2) What bias might the second article have regarding the town's budget?

☐ A preference for educational spending

☐ A bias towards environmental issues

☐ An opposition to any new projects

☐ A focus on technological advancements

8.3) What critical reading skill does Maya practice in her assignment?

☐ Speed reading

☐ Focusing only on her own opinion

☐ Identifying authors' biases and assumptions

☐ Memorizing facts from the articles

8.4) How does Maya evaluate the arguments in the articles?

☐ Based on her friends' opinions

☐ Based on evidence presented

☐ Based on the popularity of the authors

☐ Based on the length of the articles

8.5) What is a key component of Maya's report?

☐ Agreeing with one of the articles

☐ Focusing only on the negatives of each viewpoint

☐ Summarizing the articles and presenting her opinion

☐ Ignoring the articles and inventing her own facts

In Greenfield High, the science club initiated a project to create a community garden. During the planning phase, Emily, a member of the club, suggested using environmentally friendly methods. She researched various sources, encountering differing opinions on the best practices for sustainability. Emily critically analyzed these texts, noticing some were influenced by commercial interests while others were based on scientific research. In her presentation to the club, she highlighted these differences, emphasizing the importance of relying on credible, unbiased information. Her approach helped the club make informed decisions, leading to a successful and sustainable garden project.

8.6) How does Emily demonstrate critical analysis in her research?

☐ By identifying commercial biases in some texts

☐ By focusing only on scientific sources

☐ By accepting all sources as equally valid

☐ By ignoring opposing viewpoints

8.7) What skill does Emily use to effectively present her findings?

☐ Avoiding details about sustainability

☐ Presenting only one perspective

☐ Using technical jargon

☐ Summarizing complex texts clearly

8.8) What was the focus of Emily's argument in her presentation?

☐ The benefits of scientific research

☐ The drawbacks of environmental sustainability

☐ The superiority of commercial methods

☐ Relying on credible, unbiased information

8.9) What does the story suggest about evaluating different sources?

☐ Scientific sources are always unreliable

☐ All sources should be accepted without question

☐ It's important to discern biases and credibility

☐ Commercial sources are more trustworthy

8.10) What outcome resulted from Emily's approach to the project?

☐ The club chose commercial methods

☐ The project led to environmental harm

☐ The club made informed decisions for the garden

☐ The project was canceled

In the town of Lakeside, a debate arose about the conservation of the local lake, which had seen declining water quality. Sam, an active member of the school's environmental club, decided to investigate. He gathered articles, scientific studies, and local opinions. Some sources advocated for immediate action citing environmental reports, while others, backed by local businesses, downplayed the concerns. Sam critically evaluated these sources, discerning facts from opinions and identifying any underlying biases. His analysis led to a comprehensive report that he presented at a town meeting, sparking a constructive discussion on sustainable solutions. Sam's efforts highlighted the importance of critical thinking in addressing environmental issues and influenced positive changes in Lakeside.

8.11) How does Sam demonstrate critical analysis in his investigation?

☐ By discerning facts from opinions

☐ By focusing solely on local opinions

☐ By accepting all sources without questioning

☐ By ignoring scientific studies

8.12) What skill does Sam use to effectively compile his report?

☐ Using technical jargon to impress others

☐ Summarizing complex information clearly

☐ Ignoring contradictory information

☐ Focusing only on environmental reports

8.13) What was the focus of Sam's argument at the town meeting?

☐ Arguing against any form of intervention

☐ Promoting local businesses

☐ Discussing sustainable solutions for the lake

☐ Downplaying environmental concerns

8.14) What does the story suggest about evaluating different sources?

☐ Scientific studies are always biased

☐ It's crucial to identify biases and assumptions

☐ Local opinions are irrelevant

☐ All sources should be treated as equally valid

8.15) What impact did Sam's report have on the community?

☐ It led to a discussion on sustainable solutions

☐ It increased pollution in the lake

☐ It caused division and conflict

☐ It was dismissed by the community

At Westwood Library, a weekly book club met to discuss classic novels. This week's focus was 'Journey to the Stars,' a science fiction novel set in a distant future. Leo, an avid reader and critical thinker, noticed that despite its futuristic setting, the novel presented ideas relevant to current social issues. During the book club meeting, Leo pointed out instances of allegory and satire in the novel, sparking a lively discussion about its underlying messages. He encouraged his peers to look beyond the surface story and explore the deeper meanings related to humanity and progress. Leo's insights led the group to appreciate the novel's complexity and its commentary on contemporary society.

8.16) How does Leo demonstrate critical thinking in the book club?

☐ By focusing only on the futuristic aspects

☐ By accepting the novel at face value

☐ By disregarding the novel's relevance

☐ By identifying allegory and satire in the novel

8.17) What skill does Leo use to engage his peers in discussion?

☐ Avoiding complex topics

☐ Encouraging a deeper analysis of the novel

☐ Ignoring the novel's themes

☐ Sticking to a literal interpretation

8.18) What was the focus of the discussion initiated by Leo?

☐ The novel's underlying messages on humanity

☐ The scientific accuracy of the novel

☐ The entertainment value of science fiction

☐ The author's writing style

8.19) What does Leo's approach suggest about interpreting literature?

☐ It's essential to look for deeper meanings

☐ Science fiction is purely fictional

☐ Classic novels have no contemporary relevance

☐ Surface-level reading is sufficient

8.20) What impact did Leo's insights have on the book club?

☐ They appreciated the novel's complexity

☐ They decided to read only modern books

☐ They disagreed with Leo's viewpoints

☐ They lost interest in the novel

The local community center hosted a weekly movie night, featuring films from around the world. This week's film was 'The Silent Echo,' a thought-provoking drama about communication in the digital age. After watching the film, Anna, a keen observer and film enthusiast, initiated a discussion group to analyze its themes. She pointed out the use of symbolism in the film's cinematography and the underlying message about the impact of technology on human interaction. Anna's analysis encouraged the group to critically evaluate the film's portrayal of social issues, leading to a deeper understanding of its artistic and cultural significance.

8.21) How does Anna demonstrate critical analysis in the discussion group?

☐ By focusing on the entertainment value of the film

☐ By ignoring the film's deeper themes

☐ By evaluating the film's symbolism and messages

☐ By only discussing the acting quality

8.22) What aspect of the film does Anna highlight to discuss social issues?

☐ The film's special effects

☐ The use of color in cinematography

☐ The historical accuracy of the setting

☐ The portrayal of technology's impact on communication

8.23) What outcome resulted from Anna's critical analysis of 'The Silent Echo'?

☐ The group disregarded the film's message

☐ A decision to watch only similar films

☐ A deeper understanding of the film's artistic value

☐ Confusion about the film's purpose

8.24) What skill is most evident in Anna's approach to film analysis?

☐ Focusing solely on technical aspects

☐ Ignoring symbolic elements

☐ Ability to memorize film scripts

☐ Skill in identifying underlying themes

8.25) What theme is most prominent in Anna's analysis of the film?

☐ The excitement of technological advancements

☐ The impact of digital communication on society

☐ The simplicity of modern life

☐ The challenge of international filmmaking

Riverdale Middle School started a new program called 'Reading the World,' where students read and discuss global news articles. For this week's session, the class focused on an article about renewable energy initiatives in various countries. Carlos, a student with a keen interest in environmental issues, noticed that the article's tone varied when discussing different countries. He brought this observation to the class discussion, highlighting how the author's choice of words could subtly influence readers' perceptions. Carlos's insight led to a meaningful conversation about media literacy, the importance of recognizing biases, and the role of language in shaping narratives. This discussion broadened the students' understanding of critical analysis in the context of global issues.

8.26) How does Carlos exhibit critical thinking in the class discussion?

☐ By focusing on unrelated topics

☐ By accepting the article's perspective without question

☐ By pointing out the varied tone in the article

☐ By agreeing with all viewpoints

8.27) What aspect of the article does Carlos highlight to discuss biases?

☐ The length of the article

☐ The author's use of language

☐ The article's publication date

☐ The images used in the article

8.28) What outcome resulted from Carlos's observation?

☐ A deeper exploration of media literacy

☐ The class disagreed with Carlos

☐ A decision to avoid global news

☐ Confusion about the topic

8.29) What skill is most evident in Carlos's approach to the news article?

☐ Ability to memorize facts

☐ Skill in identifying language cues and biases

☐ Focusing solely on environmental aspects

☐ Ignoring the global context

8.30) What theme is most prominent in Carlos's analysis of the article?

☐ The simplicity of environmental solutions

☐ The challenge of understanding complex topics

☐ The excitement of learning new information

☐ The role of language in shaping narratives

In the local youth club, a discussion group was formed to talk about climate change and its representation in media. This week, they analyzed a documentary titled 'Our Changing Planet.' Jade, a member of the group with a passion for environmental science, noticed that the documentary presented a mix of scientific data and personal anecdotes. She led a discussion on how this combination affected the documentary's message, encouraging her peers to differentiate between empirical evidence and emotional appeal. Jade's keen analysis helped the group understand the complexity of climate change communication and the importance of a balanced approach in conveying scientific information.

8.31) How does Jade demonstrate critical thinking in the discussion group?

☐ By analyzing the mix of data and anecdotes

☐ By accepting all information as fact

☐ By only focusing on the scientific data

☐ By disregarding the documentary's message

8.32) What aspect of the documentary does Jade highlight to discuss communication?

☐ The background music used

☐ The documentary's length

☐ The balance between empirical evidence and emotional appeal

☐ The quality of the filmmaking

8.33) What outcome resulted from Jade's analysis of the documentary?

☐ Confusion about scientific data

☐ The group dismissed climate change

☐ A better understanding of climate change communication

☐ The group only focused on personal anecdotes

8.34) What skill is most evident in Jade's approach to the documentary?

☐ Focusing solely on environmental activism

☐ Ignoring the scientific aspects

☐ Skill in identifying communication strategies

☐ Ability to memorize facts

8.35) What theme is most prominent in Jade's discussion about the documentary?

☐ The challenge of filmmaking

☐ The importance of balanced scientific communication

☐ The simplicity of understanding climate change

☐ The entertainment value of documentaries

The annual science fair at Oakwood School was an event where students showcased innovative projects. This year, the theme was 'The Future of Transportation.' Nina, a student with a flair for engineering, presented a project on electric vehicles (EVs). Before the fair, she prepared by reading various articles and studies on EVs. She noticed some sources were overly optimistic, highlighting only the advantages, while others were overly critical, focusing on the challenges. In her presentation, Nina critically analyzed these perspectives, discussing both the potential and the limitations of EVs. Her balanced approach not only impressed the judges but also educated her peers about the importance of evaluating sources and considering multiple viewpoints in scientific discourse.

ALEXANDER-GRACE EDUCATION

8.36) How does Nina demonstrate critical thinking in her project preparation?

☐ By only using sources that support her view

☐ By critically analyzing differing perspectives on EVs

☐ By focusing on unrelated topics

☐ By avoiding technical details

8.37) What aspect of the sources does Nina highlight in her presentation?

☐ The reliability of the authors

☐ The length of the articles

☐ The complexity of the language used

☐ The balance between optimism and criticism

8.38) What outcome resulted from Nina's balanced approach in the science fair?

☐ Her project was disqualified

☐ She educated her peers about evaluating sources

☐ She won the first prize

☐ Her peers ignored her presentation

8.39) What skill is most evident in Nina's approach to her project on EVs?

☐ Technical engineering skills

☐ Critical analysis of various viewpoints

☐ Expertise in environmental science

☐ Ability to build complex models

8.40) What theme is most prominent in Nina's project presentation?

☐ The challenges of public speaking

☐ The ease of understanding new technology

☐ The significance of scientific debate

☐ The future is unpredictable

ALEXANDER-GRACE EDUCATION

Topic 8 – Answers

Question Number	Answer	Explanation
8.1	By emphasizing health and recreational benefits	The first article persuades readers by focusing on the health and recreational benefits a new park would bring.
8.2	A preference for educational spending	The second article shows a bias towards spending the budget on improving schools, indicating a preference in this area.
8.3	Identifying authors' biases and assumptions	Maya practices critical reading skills by identifying biases and assumptions in the articles she researches.
8.4	Based on evidence presented	Maya evaluates the arguments based on the evidence presented in the articles.
8.5	Summarizing the articles and presenting her opinion	Maya's report includes summarizing the articles and presenting her own opinion on the matter.
8.6	By identifying commercial biases in some texts	Emily demonstrates critical analysis by identifying commercial biases in some of the texts she researches.
8.7	Summarizing complex texts clearly	Emily effectively presents her findings by summarizing complex texts in a clear and understandable manner.
8.8	Relying on credible, unbiased information	Emily's argument focuses on the importance of relying on credible, unbiased information for the garden project.
8.9	It's important to discern biases and credibility	The story suggests the importance of evaluating different sources based on their biases and credibility.
8.10	The club made informed decisions for the garden	Emily's approach leads to the club making informed decisions for the community garden project.
8.11	By discerning facts from opinions	Sam demonstrates critical analysis by distinguishing between factual information and opinions in his research.
8.12	Summarizing complex information clearly	Sam uses the skill of summarizing complex information clearly in compiling his report.
8.13	Discussing sustainable solutions for the lake	At the town meeting, Sam focuses on discussing sustainable solutions for the lake's conservation.
8.14	It's crucial to identify biases and assumptions	The story suggests the importance of recognizing biases and assumptions when evaluating different sources.
8.15	It led to a discussion on sustainable solutions	Sam's report sparks a constructive discussion on sustainable solutions in the community.
8.16	By identifying allegory and satire in the novel	Leo demonstrates critical thinking by recognizing allegory and satire in the novel during the book club meeting.
8.17	Encouraging a deeper analysis of the novel	Leo engages his peers by encouraging them to delve deeper into the novel's themes and meanings.
8.18	The novel's underlying messages on humanity	The focus of the discussion initiated by Leo is on the novel's underlying messages about humanity.

8.19	It's essential to look for deeper meanings	Leo's approach suggests the importance of interpreting literature by looking for deeper meanings and themes.
8.20	They appreciated the novel's complexity	Leo's insights lead the book club to appreciate the complexity and deeper messages of the novel.
8.21	By evaluating the film's symbolism and messages	Anna demonstrates critical analysis by focusing on the film's symbolism and underlying messages.
8.22	The portrayal of technology's impact on communication	Anna highlights the film's portrayal of technology's impact on communication and its effects on society.
8.23	A deeper understanding of the film's artistic value	Anna's critical analysis of 'The Silent Echo' leads to a deeper understanding of its artistic and cultural significance.
8.24	Skill in identifying underlying themes	Anna's skill in identifying the film's underlying themes and messages is evident in her analysis.
8.25	The impact of digital communication on society	Anna's analysis of the film reveals a theme focused on the impact of digital communication on society.
8.26	By pointing out the varied tone in the article	Carlos exhibits critical thinking by observing the varied tone used in the global news article.
8.27	The author's use of language	Carlos highlights the author's use of language as a way to discuss biases present in the article.
8.28	A deeper exploration of media literacy	Carlos's observation leads to a meaningful conversation about media literacy in the classroom.
8.29	Skill in identifying language cues and biases	Carlos's ability to identify language cues and biases is a key skill demonstrated in his approach to the article.
8.30	The role of language in shaping narratives	Carlos's analysis of the article focuses on the theme of how language can shape narratives and perceptions.
8.31	By analyzing the mix of data and anecdotes	Jade demonstrates critical thinking by evaluating the blend of scientific data and personal stories in the documentary.
8.32	The balance between empirical evidence and emotional appeal	Jade highlights how the documentary balances empirical evidence with emotional appeal in its communication.
8.33	A better understanding of climate change communication	Jade's analysis results in a more comprehensive understanding of climate change communication among the group.
8.34	Skill in identifying communication strategies	Jade's skill in identifying various communication strategies is evident in her approach to analyzing the documentary.
8.35	The importance of balanced scientific communication	The discussion led by Jade reveals the theme of the importance of balanced communication in scientific topics.
8.36	By critically analyzing differing perspectives on EVs	Nina demonstrates critical thinking by evaluating various viewpoints on electric vehicles.
8.37	The balance between optimism and criticism	Nina highlights the balance between optimistic and critical perspectives in the sources she analyzed.
8.38	She educated her peers about evaluating sources	Nina's balanced approach educates her peers about the importance of evaluating sources in scientific discourse.
8.39	Critical analysis of various viewpoints	Nina's skill in critically analyzing different viewpoints is evident in her approach to the EV project.
8.40	The significance of scientific debate	Nina's project presentation focuses on the theme of the significance of scientific debate, especially in new technologies.

Ready for More?

The NWEA MAP testing is adaptive. This means that if your student found these questions too tricky or too easy, they may find it useful to practice grades below or above they grade they are in. This will expose students to new concepts and ideas, giving them a better chance at scoring higher in tests.

Alexander-Grace Education produces books covering Mathematics, Sciences, and English, to help your student maximize their potential in these areas.

For errata, please email
alexandergraceeducation@gmail.com

Made in the USA
Las Vegas, NV
27 December 2024